T0368173

THE
CROSS COUNTRY
Honey Moon

THE
CROSS COUNTRY
Honey Moon

MARY ELIZABETH MORTON

To order additional copies of this book, contact:
Xlibris
844-714-8691
www.Xlibris.com
Orders@Xlibris.com
822998

Contents

Forward

The purpose of my book is to relate the experiences of my grandmother's early life as it has been told to me all of my life. I have written it in the first person just as she told it to me. She had so many unique and interesting experiences that it would be a waste for her life story not to be told. This story is being written in order for others to enjoy the humorous as well as heart rending episodes that make life a heartwarming experience for everyone who chooses to share her story.

My grandmother, Elizabeth Greenlee Baldwin, was raised on a farm in the mountains of North Carolina. She entered nurse's training in July, 1907, at the Knoxville General Hospital in Knoxville, Tennessee, graduating three years later as a Registered Nurse. Training back in those days meant from 12-18 hours or more per day with only a half a day off each week.

After her graduation from training, my grandmother married Dr. John Bronough Baldwin, a country doctor from Nicholasville, Kentucky, and served as his nurse. After fifteen months of practice in Coal Creek or (Lake City), Tennessee, my grandfather developed a tubercular condition and was advised to go west to the vicinity of Denver, Colorado, to seek restoration of his health.

There began a very adventuresome journey as they made the trip in a Studebaker, Hug-me-tight buggy drawn by a Kentucky thoroughbred who was the great grandson of the famous racehorse, Dan Patch. Dan Patch won the Kentucky Derby in Lexington, Kentucky in 1903 for harness racing.

As luggage space on a buggy is limited, my grandparents had a metal box constructed to fit behind the buggy seat into which were placed supplies essential for the trip such as a pound of flour, a pound of sugar, lard, etc.

They left Coal Creek on May 3, 1915, and arrived in Denver on August 4. Their experiences in route are very interesting and unusual. For example, they camped by the roadside or in open pastures at night and were never free from terrible thunderstorms or wild animals. One night my grandparents returned to their campsite to find a big sow in the middle of my grandmother's cot. Another time the wind blew over the sterno stove catching the cot on fire.

After spending a year in Denver where my grandfather underwent surgery, they began the second leg of their journey from Denver, Colorado, to Roswell, New Mexico, where my mother was born. Here, they stayed until my grandfather's death in 1918, after returning to North Carolina where she began a nursing career which was to last for sixty years until 1967. She retired and owned her own home in Albemarle, North Carolina until her death in 1983.

Introduction

When I was around sixteen years old, my father sent me from my home in Greenlee, N. C. to Concord to boarding school. This was called the Laura Sunderland School for Girls and was run by the Northern Presbyterian Church. It was only the second time I had been on a train and the second time I had been on a trip all alone. I traveled from Greenlee to Salisbury, N.C. and then from Salisbury to Concord.

Greenlee is a very small community which is located in McDowell County between Old Fort and Marion, N.C. My father, Ephraim Leland Leonard Greenlee, was a farmer and a saw mill man. He owned a saw mill and had sawed the lumber that went to build the Vanderbilt mansion in Asheville, N.C. He was a very intelligent man who read Greek and Latin. As a young man he had attended Dr. Foster's School for Young Gentlemen located in Lenoir, N.C. He was a good, kind person and always had time for heart to heart talks with his children.

I was Harriett Elizabeth Greenlee. My family called me "Bess" for short. I had six brothers and sisters all of whom were younger than I. There was: Francis Leland, James McDowell, Thomas Leonard, whom we called Jack, Charlotte Lenoir, Mary Catherine, whom we called Polly, and Dorothy McIntosh, or Dot. I had always considered the scenery around Greenlee, N. C. to be the most beautiful in the world. I loved my mountains, two of which my great grandfather had at one time owned, and one of these mountains was named Greenlee after us. He had not only owned two mountains, but he had owned a wide track of land which had been acquired as a land grant when his family first settled here. This land grant stretched from Greenlee to somewhere beyond Morganton, N.C.

After arriving at school, I was immediately given my schedule which I was to follow. All students had part of the day for school and part for work. The girls took turns working in the kitchen, in the laundry, in the sewing room, and cleaning the teacher's room. Everyone's work was changed every six weeks. But, it seemed to me that my turn came to scrub the kitchen floor quicker than any other duty.

I was especially good in history. The best history student was awarded a beautiful broach to wear as long as she kept her grades up, and I had the honor of wearing it the whole time I was in school there. This broach had a picture of Laura Sunderland in the center and was surrounded by pearls.

My mother, Katie May Dover Greenlee, had attended the Asheville Normal and I had the same teacher that she had had, Miss Melissa Montgomery. Miss Montgomery was a wonderful woman but a strict disciplinarian.

About The Author

I was born in Albemarle, N.C. and graduated from Albemarle High School
in 1963. I attended the University of N.C. at Greensboro for four years and
graduated in 1967 with a B.A. Degree in Speech Pathology and Audiology.
After teaching as a speech therapist in the schools for six years I entered graduate
school at the University of N.C. at Greensboro in 1973. And finished with a
Master of Education Degree in speech communication in August, 1975.
I taught as a speech therapist in the Charlotte Mecklenburg Schools for 2 yrs (1967-
1970) and in the Chesterfield County Public Schools in Virginia from 1970-1973.
I attended the University of S.C. in Columbia from 1977-
1978 where I studied speech pathology and audiology.
I wrote my book while I was in graduate school years before
I met Jim Huneycutt. I met Jim in the 1990's.

─── *Years In Training* ───

In June I came home, but I felt that I had to have some other type of work to do, or I would have to go to the field to help my father with the corn and beans, etc. I didn't think that I would like that as my life's work. Therefore, I put in my application to attend nurse's training at the Old Knoxville General Hospital in Knoxville, Tennessee. In June, 1907, I was accepted to begin my training in July. I had to take the train, old #12 to Asheville. Then, I would change to the one from S.C. which was called the Carolina Special. I was to take the Carolina Special from Asheville to Knoxville.

I was 5'2" tall with fair complexion, dark hair and hazel eyes. My dark hair was pulled back out of my eyes and tied with a big red bow at the back of my head. From there it hung loose around my shoulders and down my back. I weighed only 95 lbs. and wore a cotton dress made by my mother. She sewed beautifully and made all her children's clothes. I carried only one suitcase.

At this time I had a boil on my bottom. As I was standing at the gate waiting for the train, a salesman came up to me, swinging his suitcase, and hit me on my backside, rupturing my boil. I felt miserable but was glad that my very painful injury didn't show.

My train arrived in Knoxville at approximately 3:00 or 4:00 PM that same day. From there I took an Oakwood streetcar and went out to the hospital. As I entered on the left hand side of the hall, I noted the superintendent's office, that of Miss Jeanette Paulus. I went in, showed her my admission slip, where upon Miss Paulus immediately called one of the other student nurses, Miss Carolyn Volena Lee, to her office. Miss Lee, who was one year ahead of me, was to take me to my room and put my hair up, as I wore my hair in long dark curls. Miss Paulus shook my hair and stated, "Please take this lady upstairs and put her hair up. We will have no babies around here." Miss Lee, who turned out to be my boss, did as she was bidden.

The next day when I went on duty for the first time, I found that Miss Lee was the head nurse. I was put on the men's colored ward. I was immediately handed a pan of soiled instruments and told to scrub them until they were clean. "When you finish scrubbing these instruments, please put them on the carriage."

However, I was not told where or what the carriage was. After I finished scrubbing the instruments, I noticed that the ambulance, pulled by two big bay horses, was located outside the back entrance to the hospital. I took the instruments out the back entrance, handed them to Charlie, the ambulance driver, and told him that these instruments had been sent to him. He thanked me as he took them from me.

The next morning Miss Lee came to me. She said, "What in the world did you do with those instruments?"

"I put them on the carriage," I said.

"Well, they are not on the carriage."

"What is the carriage?" I asked. She then took me aside and showed me a table on wheels where the surgical instruments, gauze, and bandages were placed. This carriage could be pushed around from patient to patient in order to change one's bandages or dressings.

"Now, don't watch me, and I'll go get them," I said.

I then went outside to speak to Charlie. I said, "Please hand me those instruments, I made a mistake. Those instruments were not supposed to be for you."

"Well, I thought you must have made a mistake because I already have the sterile instruments that belong in the ambulance."

No one ever knew where those instruments were put. When I went back to Knoxville for a reunion thirty years later, everyone was asking me where I had put those instruments that day.

I had six months on the men's colored ward, six months on the white men's ward, and three months on night duty. Then, in the Fall of 1908, a new intern arrived for training. His name was Dr. John Bronaugh Baldwin. He was very tall, 6'7" tall to be exact, with black straight hair, which was cut short in the back and longer in front. He wore a part on the left side of his head. His eyes were hazel colored and everyone talked about how good looking the new intern was. Since he only weighed 175 lbs., everyone called him "high pockets." The girls teased me and told me that if I didn't watch out, I would be getting me a new fellow. They were going to try to catch him first.

Later, I was to learn that as a young boy John had attended a private school in Russellville, Kentucky. He was a graduate of The University of the South in Swanee, Tennessee, and of the University of Maryland Medical School in Baltimore. He had also studied for a year at the John Hopkins Medical School before he started his internship at the Knoxville General Hospital..

One day I was walking down the hall and I passed the intern's lounge when I heard the new intern say, "What's that girl's name?"

The other doctor said, "Why that's Miss Greenlee."

"Well, she might be Miss Greenlee to you, but she but she looks like a baby doll to me." I was his baby doll as long as he lived. After we married, it was shortened to "Babe." I called him J.B. The new superintendent of the hospital was Dr. J.B. Johnson as there had been a city election since I had entered training, and Miss Paulus had resigned. I called John J.B. so that if anyone heard me speaking of J.B., they would be misled into thinking that I was talking about the superintendent instead of my sweetheart.

Student nurses and interns were not allowed to date, although J.B. had been accused of going out with one of the student nurses. The nurse had been taken off the hall and was being punished. She had been seen with him at the drug store. He later told me that he was in the drug store, and as she came in, he was going out. He greeted her and held the door for her as he left. Someone saw them and reported to the superintendent that Dr. Baldwin had been dating one of the nurses.

Everyone that was on night duty always ate together around midnight. We called this our "midnight supper." Many times Dr. Baldwin would join me for meals at this time. He was only here approximately a year.

In the spring of 1909, he left to open a practice in Coal Creek, Tennessee, which is now called Lake City. This small town is in the Norris Dam vicinity and was located approximately thirty miles away. He was to be a coal mine doctor for the men who worked in the coal mines as well as their families.

At times he would call me and ask me to catch the train and meet him in Clinton, Tennessee. He always came by horse and buggy and we would have a nice afternoon together.

One night before I graduated, while I was on night duty, there was a death on our floor. The boy from the Donahue and Hall Funeral Home, Harry, came in to take the man's body away. But, before he could get to the men's ward, he had to pass the colored ward. Previously to this, I had been trying to convince an old skinny colored woman, Margaret, to move from the front to the back of the ward, as she refused to keep her bed straightened. I was always being scolded by my supervisor for Margaret's unkept bed, since it was the first bed in the ward. Margaret had always refused to keep the sheet over her. Every time I passed the door, I would go in the ward and straighten the sheet on her bed. I suppose she thought it was too hot that summer for cover. I would say, "Now, you just have to keep your sheet over you."

Well, as Harry approached to door, he asked me, "Where is the corpse?"

I answered, "Right in here." He moved up to Margaret's bed where she was sleeping with the sheet pulled over her head. Suddenly, without a word he jerked the sheet off of the bed. Margaret jumped up and threw her hands up in the air and shouted, "Lawdy mercy!" I think it frightened Harry about as much as it did Margaret. Just at that moment the hall telephone rang. It was located outside the door and began ringing and ringing. As I answered the phone, I heard the supervisor scream, "What's the matter?" "What's the matter down there?"

"Oh, it's just Margaret. It isn't anything. Everything is just fine." I knew we had disturbed the peace at 2:00A.M. But, Harry had always been teasing me; so, I thought that at last I was even with him. But, the next day I found that Margaret had moved to the back of the ward and was a model patient from then on.

After I was married, Harry told me that if I ever had trouble finding a casket long enough for my husband, as he was 6'7" tall, he would be glad to supply one and help me out. Only, this was said in jest.

The superintendent of nurses, Miss Lillian Burgin, was a cousin of mine. One day her brother, Edward, came to see her. We had played together as children and were good friends. I was two months older than he was.

One afternoon she called me to her office and told me that she would give me the afternoon off if I would take Edward downtown and show him around. I did, and that night I was to be on night duty. I told him, "When I go to supper, I'll come up and tap on the door. Then, you can have supper with us." We had bananas, buttered toast sandwiches, and hot chocolate. I picked up the bananas and put them in the old fashioned ice box. When we finished supper, we had iced bananas for dessert.

The next morning I met Lillian coming out of the dining room. She said, "Did you know that brother was ill last night? He was terribly sick. I had to give him a dose of castor oil. He just vomited and vomited. What in the world did you eat yesterday while you were out?"

I answered, "Well, we went to Kilman's Drug Store and had ice cream sodas and something to drink. I can't think of anything we ate that would have made him ill." I purposely did not mention to Lillian that Ed had eaten midnight supper with us, as it would have been against the rules.

It wasn't until years later that we told her that the iced bananas had made Edward ill that night. That was the last time I had put bananas on ice before eating them. They didn't make me ill, but I was used to them.

Lee asked one night if I'd like to go to town with her. We would meet her boyfriend, A. Pullus, and go to dinner at Mitchell's Café which was located beside Kulman's Drug Store. We were all having such a nice time. I even drank my first beer. When suddenly, someone turned around and happened to see the clock. There was a large clock on the wall behind us. I screamed, "Oh, my Lord, we're late!" I jumped up so quickly that I knocked the chair over. There were restrictions on girls back then, and we had to be in before Midnight. We left as quickly as we could. The buses also stopped running at Midnight; therefore, we had to walk home past the Federal Cemetery. This way no one would see us. Pulllus walked with us. This cemetery is lined with beautiful magnolia trees, and I always considered it the most beautiful spot in Knoxville, but only in the daytime.

When we went in, Dr. Johnson was in the office. Lee, who was the daughter of a prominent physician, walked right in with her head high, and I slipped by her and went upstairs. The next morning one of the supervisors came to my room to tell me that I was to stay in my room until someone came to give me a scolding. I was to stay there for two weeks when I was not in class or on duty. I was not allowed to go outside at all. They always assigned unpleasant duties for punishment. My punishment was night duty and Lee was assigned to the operating room.

One night while I was still on night duty, I went to the kitchen for some bread as the food wagon was short by one loaf. I was looking through some five gallon cans for the bread when I found a tiny little mouse in the bottom of one of the cans. He was too small to climb out. I caught him and took him back to the women's ward where we were having dinner. Later, several other nurses and I tied him up in an adhesive box, put brown paper around it, tied a string around the box, addressed it, glued a cancelled stamp on it, and placed it on Miss Burgin's desk. The next morning she found a gift. Someone told me that when she opened the box, her scream could be heard all over the hospital. She was so frightened that she jumped to the top of her desk, so I heard.

In the spring Harry Houdini came to Knoxville. It was advertised in the newspapers and on posters which had been placed in store windows around town that the "Human Fly," Harry Houdini, would scale the tallest building in Knoxville. Several of us who were on night duty went to town to see the spectacle.

In June, 1910, approximately one month before I graduated, Dr. J.B. Johnson, the superintendent of the hospital, called me to his office. He said that he had received a call from a friend of his in Newport, Tennessee, who wanted a nurse for a seriously ill patient. He asked me whether I could be ready in time to leave for Newport that afternoon. I answered, "Yes." My uniforms were all ready. It was late when the train arrived in Newport. The man was extremely ill with typhoid and died before daylight. Therefore, I returned to Knoxville on the afternoon train. Dr. Johnson called me to his office and I stated, "The man died a few hours after I arrived to care for him. He only lived six or seven hours."

"Did you get your money?"

"I didn't charge him anything," I said.

"What! Well you'll never make a living like that."

"Well, I couldn't charge him anything because he died. I didn't do much for him except bathe him and get him ready for the undertaker."

"Don't do that anymore," said Dr. Johnson. "Be sure and charge even if you were only there an hour."

Dr. Johnson later told all the other doctors and they constantly teased me about it. They all said that I was the kind of nurse that they would like to have. They could save money.

In those days, the Knoxville General was a city hospital. Instead of having a designated time for classes to begin in the Fall as most schools do today, the girls entering training could begin anytime during the year. They attended school all year round for three years until they had completed the academic and practical work that was assigned to them. When they had completed their programs, each was called to Dr. Johnson's office where she was awarded her diploma. The diploma was signed by the doctors and city officials.

I finally completed my course work as well as practical work and passed the State Board of Examiners for Nurses of the state of Tennessee on July 13, 1910. There were no graduation exercises in those days. I was called to Dr. Johnson's office to receive my diploma on July 15, 1910. At last I was officially a Registered Nurse in the State of Tennessee.

During the final months of my nurses training, I began making plans. I would continue to do special duty with individual cases. I was not hired by a hospital as nurses are today. In the meantime, three of my classmates and myself rented a two bedroom unfurnished apartment together. The others were: Carolyn Volena Lee, Mary Lou Pendegrass, and Alameda Harrison. The apartment had two bedrooms, a living room, and a bath. Since there was no kitchen, we converted the bathroom into a kitchen by putting the ironing board over the bathtub for a table. We purchased a small wire box to put in the window for the purpose of holding supplies such as bread and butter, and we used the window as an ice box.

This apartment, the Hobbs, as it was called, was a four or five story brick building. It was located on Market Street. Our apartment was on the first floor. One could walk down Market Street about a half a block and enter the fish stalls of the Farmer's Market. This market was a block square and was considered to be one of the most wonderful markets anywhere around. One could buy such delicious foods, including pastries and breads as well as beautiful flowers.

We bought an electric hot plate which we put on a board and placed on the radiator in the bathroom. This was out stove. Mostly, the apartment was furnished with second hand furniture, and each person contributed something.

── A Nurse at Last ──

The first case to which I was assigned after graduation was in Jonesboro. The man was seriously injured in a railroad accident and needed special nursing care. I caught the train to Johnson City where a member of the man's family met me and took me to Jonesboro. The patient was a brakeman for the railroad and had accidentally cut his leg off while on duty.

This was the first time I had ever been out of the "sticks," and I was there about a week. He would say, "Miss Greenlee, my toe hurts," or "Please move my leg. I have the cramp in my foot," or "Would you put something under my heel?" I always adjusted the cover as he asked, pretending the foot was still there. It was the physician's responsibility to inform the patient that his leg had been amputated when he felt that the patient was well enough to withstand the emotional shock of such a traumatic experience. He could possibly go into hysterics and die from shock.

On Sunday, one of the patient's friends took me to a foot washing Baptist Church. I had never seen anything like this before. The women washed the other women's feet, and the men washed the men's feet. They sang and shouted as they moved through the aisles.

The next case to which I was assigned was a man with typhoid in Copperhill, Tennessee. J.B. (John) came down from Coal Creek to tell me that he wanted to get married right away. I told him that I couldn't get married now. I couldn't leave my patient. The patient died later on. It wasn't until we were married that he told me why he had been in such a hurry to get married that day. He had had a job offer, but the physician they were to hire had to be married.

After I graduated, J.B. was still working hard, and I was doing private duty. One day I had a case up beyond Johnson City. It was located out in the country next to a grocery store. After I had been there several days, the store clerk came to me and said, "Miss Greenlee, you have a long distance telephone call."

I went over and picked up the receiver. Central said, "Dr. Baldwin, here's your baby doll."

I answered, "Who was that calling me baby doll?"

"That was my friend, central." Central would hunt me up anywhere I was. I was always his baby doll.

Then, in the Fall of 1912, the Southern Appalachian Fair came to Chilhowee Park in Knoxville. I sent Daddy enough money to bring my brothers, Jim and Leland, who were 12 and 14 years of age. They had never been to such a large fair before. The ones we had at home in Greenlee were very small and never even had an elephant.

The fair always had a first aid station in case of accidents. Some people become ill while attending large events. So, our hospital provided the nurses for the first aid station, and the hospital across the street provided the doctors. I had received a call asking me to be one of the nurses, and I agreed to do this.

Each station consisted of a wooden platform covered by canvas. During the three weeks that the fair was to be in Knoxville, William Cody, better known as Buffalo Bill, Annie Oakley, and others including cowboys and Indians put on their Wild West Show for the public twice a day. The cowboys did rope tricks, sharp shooting, and fancy riding.

Daddy and the boys spent three wonderful days and nights in Knoxville and had a delightful time. While they were there, I bought them their first long pants of which they were so proud.

Sometime later, I contracted a bad sore throat with a cough, and I went to Dr. Malcolm G. Hall (Harrison's boyfriend). He told me that I needed to have my tonsils out. I called J.B. and asked him to please come over and give me the anesthetic. Harrison went with me to his office. After they put me to sleep, I stopped breathing, and they had to work quickly to revive me. When I awoke, J. B. said, "You know, you just about scared the life out of us." Dr. Hall said, "You took half of my life just then. You scared me half to death." Harrison and I went back to our apartment. Then during the middle of the night, I started bleeding. The fright he experienced that afternoon was being drowned in a bottle. My roommates finally reached Dr. Luttrell who came and put another stitch in. J.B. told me later that there would have been a big to do over this incident if I had died.

After my throat healed, I began coughing again. Dr. Hall told me that I should go home for a much needed rest. I had also lost quite a bit of weight. He wanted me to drink raw eggs in sherry. So, Lee's boy friend, A. Pullus, sent me a whole case of sherry. Mother would pour a tea cup full of sherry, drop a raw egg in it, and give it to me to drink.

While I was recuperating at home, J.B. came to meet my family. Our house was built around a chimney. There were three rooms downstairs and three rooms upstairs. Each room had a large fireplace. We would sit in the parlor, and my two sisters, Dot and Polly, who were approximately ages seven and nine respectively, would peek around the corner and just giggle.

One night Daddy came in with a Civil War sword and saber that had been brought back from the war by his half-brother, David Greenlee. He pulled the sword out from the saber and said, "Doctor, what is your politics?"

He answered, "I am from Kentucky." That was all he had to say. In those days Kentucky was all Democratic, and Daddy didn't want a Republican sitting in front of his fire.

When he went back to Knoxville, I went with him as far as Asheville, N.C. He took me to dinner, and he ordered rare steaks. When they brought them, they looked raw. He said to the waiter, "I like rare steaks, but these are just a little too rare." The waiter then took them back to the kitchen and cooked them a little more. While we were eating, J.B. looked up and said, "Now, this would be a good time, let's go get married."

I answered, "I can't now. I just can't. I didn't bring any clothes with me. I hadn't planned on getting married."

J.B. said, "Well, I'll surprise you some day." After dinner I went to the train station with him, as his train came in before mine. He went back to Knoxville, and I went back home to Greenlee.

When I arrived back home, Mother said, "Well, I didn't expect you. I thought maybe you would go with the doctor."

In the Fall of 1913, I received a call from the King's Daughter's Hospital in Middlesboro, Kentucky, saying that they needed a hall nurse for the winter. Therefore, I went. I had been there approximately one week. It was on a Sunday afternoon around 6:00 P.M. when I received word that I had a long distance telephone call. I immediately rose from the dining room table where I was eating to go to answer the phone. It was J.B. He said, "I want you to be in Coal Creek in the morning. You go to Corbin, Kentucky tonight. In the morning you take the L & N at 6:00 A. M., and I'll meet you at the train station in Coal Creek at 8:00 A. M."

"Look here, I can't do that. I promised to work here all winter. I signed a contract."

"To Hell with that. Come over here and I'll give you a life time job."

So, I went to the office and told the superintendent that I had had an important call and that I had to leave. I caught the train and went to Corbin where I spent the night in a hotel. The next morning I arose in time to catch the L & N. J.B. was there to meet me when I arrived in Coal Creek at 8:00A.M.

The doctor had a patient in his office on whom he was going to operate that day. He performed a hysterectomy on Mrs. Turner in his office. He then made her comfortable in his bedroom and had set up a cot in his office for Mr. Turner. J.B. had planned to go to a hotel. He had also hired a cook who had agreed to stay as long as she was needed.

J.B. had rented a small house containing two large rooms and two small rooms with a porch. One large room the doctor used as an office with a connecting waiting room. The two smaller rooms were used as a kitchen and bedroom.

Two or three days later an engineer from the L & N Railroad had his leg accidently cut off as he was working. J.B. called Lee and asked her to come over to help us. We operated on him to try to stop the bleeding; but, the man died sometime during the night. The next day Lee said, "Now, this would be a good time for you to get married."

"All right," I said. We dressed up. I put on my best hobbled skirt, and we went to the train station. J.B. was helping me up the steps of the train when I met Dr. Horn, one of the handsome young doctors who lived in Coal Creek. He spoke and lifted his hat as he stepped down from the train. I went on in and sat down next to a window. Well, as Dr. Baldwin came in and sat down beside me he was swearing. He said that I had been smiling and flirting with his worst enemy. Oh, he was so angry.

So, I decided why should I marry him if he was going to go into a rage every time I spoke to a man. I said, "I don't want to get married now," and he replied, "I wouldn't marry you on a Christmas tree."

After we arrived in Clinton he said that he had to go to the Court House. I said, "You needn't go to buy a license. I'm not going to marry you, now."

He replied, "You needn't worry. I'm not going to buy a license." I was crying so hard that I had to borrow 50 cents from J.B. to buy a handkerchief to dry my tears.

We returned to Coal Creek to a supper which Lee had prepared for our wedding dinner. When we walked in Lee asked, "Well, did you get married?"

The doctor said, "Not this time."

After supper J.B. said, "Let's all go up to the drug store. George Turner can take care of his wife." Dr. Rome Stansberry, the druggist, came over to get our order. He said to me, "Well, is it Mrs. Baldwin?"

I answered, "No, not yet."

J.B. asked, "What do you suppose she means, Rome?"

Coal Creek

The next morning was Tuesday, November, 11, 1913. J.B. took Lee to the train station for her return trip to Knoxville. He called me from the station and told me that he was going to the mountains to see a patient. "When I return," he said, "I want you to go to Dutch Valley with me to see a typhoid patient." I told him of course I would go with him.

It rained all day. Mrs. Price, the cook, asked me if she could go home early. Some of her children were ill. I told her that I would finish supper for her, and I was trying to carve a chicken that she had cooked when the doctor walked in carrying the mail. I looked up and said, "I can't cut this chicken," and he answered me, "To Hell with that chicken, come on let's get married."

I said, "Why, of course I'm ready." I didn't think he could get the license or the preacher, so I said, "All right."

Then, he pulled the license out of one pocket and the ring out of his watch pocket, and said, "The preacher is next door."

Early that morning he had called Harrison and asked her to go downtown to buy a wedding ring for him. As his mother's wedding ring had worn into, he wanted a ring that would last a hundred years.

I pulled off my cap and went across the street to Dr. Stansberry's house where a Baptist minister, Mr. Duncan, married us. The doctor said to the preacher, "Pastor, I'm sorry that I have to leave so soon, but I have a woman in labor. I'll have to be in a hurry." We said our vows. Then, J.B. kissed me, shook hands with everyone, took me back to the office, and left for the labor case. He had left Mrs. Johnson about 6:00 P.M., after administering some morphine to quiet her pains until he could come down to Coal Creek and get married.

The phone rang about 2:00 A.M., and I answered it. The woman on the other end of the line said, "Who's speaking?" When I answered, "This is Mrs. Baldwin," a voice on the other end of the phone said, "It must be true." The doctor had told his patient and the other people who happened to be with him that he was married while he was gone. They hadn't believed him.

The next morning J.B. came in and said that he was dead for sleep; so we made up the cot. He went to sleep in his office. He stayed there all day. I made supper and took care of Mrs. Turner. Then, that night the doctor had to go back to the hotel to spend the night.

Mrs. Turner was with us for a couple of weeks before she was well enough to go home to Dutch Valley. Then, J.B. and I started on a trip to Middlesboro, Kentucky by the Southern Railroad to visit his mother. The doctor could not leave his patients long enough for a trip anywhere else.

We left Coal Creek around 3:00 P.M. The train pulled into the station at Cumberland Gap around 6:00P.M. and stopped. A short extremely fat man covered with black coal dust came down the aisle of the train and sat down beside me. When I moved over to keep him from touching me, he laughed and said, "I'm your little brother, Louis. Most people call me "Bunny." John is afraid to go through the tunnel; so, he's going to walk over the mountain." Then, I looked up and saw John coming down the aisle. They both laughed as they thought that they had a great joke on me.

I learned that Bunny worked for the L & N Railroad weighing coal which explains why he was covered with coal dust. He loved to go coon hunting, and he had lots of hunting dogs. The railroad had even issued him a pass signed by the superintendent of the L & N Railroad which said, "L.D. Baldwin and his dogs." He and his dogs could ride anywhere he wanted to go for free.

When we arrived at the train station in Middlesboro, J.B., Bunny, and I took a surrey to his mother's house. Upon arrival, I saw a big white two story wooden framed house on top of a steep hill overlooking the town. There was a large front porch and several tall trees out in front of the house. I found a wonderful welcome from his mother and his sister-in-law, Mamie. Mamie was the wife of John's older brother, Nat. Mamie had also brought his eight month old baby girl, Eunice May with her from Osceola, Arkansas, where she and Nat lived. Nat and his father-in-law, Mr. Andrew Johnson, owned a large cotton plantation. We found a warm welcome and a delicious dinner waiting for us, and from then on, I was treated as if I had always been a member of the family.

We stayed three or four days and then went home to Coal Creek to find my new home painted on the inside. Our bedroom was painted pink. The office, waiting room, and kitchen were painted white. On the wall of the freshly painted bedroom, we found a black hand print. One of the coal miners had been passing by and had left the imprint of his hand on the wall. We found a beautiful new white and black coal and wood range in the kitchen. It had a warming oven and a reservoir for hot water on the side of the stove.

Upon our return to Coal Creek, we also found a letter from my father. He had received the announcement of my marriage and was writing congratulations from the family. Previously, he and I had discussed his moving the family to Knoxville. There my brother and sisters would have a chance to attend better schools. In the letter he told me the exact date that they planned to arrive in Knoxville. That date was somewhere around the end of November.

Later that afternoon, J.B. went to Watt's Grocery Store where he purchased, not only food, but a set of blue willow dishes, pots, and pans. Mother Baldwin, as she had requested me to call her Mother, had given John the furniture from his room at home in Nicholasville. Her given name was Nancy Rebecca Bronaugh, and most people called her Miss Nanny. John and his one sister and four brothers had been raised in Nicholasville, Kentucky. There was: Mary, Nathaniel Bronaugh, Rodney Haggard, Louis Doyle, Jr. or Bunny, and Wheeler. At this time, Mother Baldwin still owned that home but kept it rented. She had given John the bed and dresser and all of the bed clothes for his bed. The brass bed and bed clothes had been especially made for him by Chatham, Inc. in Elkin, N.C., as he was 6'7" tall and had difficulty finding one long enough. J.B. and his brother, Wheeler, wore the same size. Wheeler had died at the age of fourteen with tuberculosis and was buried in Nicholasville. This is a lovely cemetery where the graves are surrounded by tall maple trees from whence it acquired its name.

J.B. also purchased two matching chairs and a rocker for me and a big arm chair for him. We had no heat except for a small grate in the bedroom fireplace which burned coal and the kitchen stove.

The next morning Mr. Underwood knocked on the door. He said that he owed J.B. $30.00 and he wanted to give him a young cow which he was leading as payment for his bill. We gratefully accepted the cow and named her Suky. She made the nicest pet and gave all the milk we needed. Not long after this another man brought us five or six pigs.

Many times I went with J.B. on calls to visit patients. He loved children and always filled his pockets full of jelly beans for them. Of course his pockets stretched out of shape from the weight of the candy. Children would come up to him saying, "Please give me some medicine." Whereupon he would reach into his pockets and dole out candy for each child saying, "Take one of these every hour." These children loved to see him come as they liked the attention he gave to them.

Near the end of November, Mother and Daddy and all my brothers and sisters arrived at the train station in Knoxville. J.B. and I were there to meet them. We all ate supper at the Adkin Hotel where we rented three rooms: one for Mother and Daddy to share with the girls, one room for the boys, and one for J.B. and me.

None of the children had been vaccinated; so, J.B. was planning to give them their shots before they began school there. Daddy rounded up all the children and brought them to our room where he proceeded to line them up. Polly and Dot were both frightened, especially Dot. Dot began running all around the room. She ran from one chair to another and around the bed while J.B. and Daddy pursued her. Finally, Dot crawled under the bed where she continued going from one end of the bed to the other. J.B. stood guard on one side of the bed and Daddy on the other. J.B. eventually pulled her out and vaccinated her in spite of screams of protest.

Polly and Jack were fascinated with the hotel elevator as they had never seen one. They kept riding it up and down and were having a great time.

The next day the doctor and Daddy spent the day house hunting. When they returned later that afternoon, Daddy said, "The doctor just about walked me to death. He takes such big steps and walks faster than any man I've ever seen." They had found a little cottage to rent on Magnolia Street. Later, the boys were able to find odd jobs after school. All three of my brothers were slender with dark curly hair and blue eyes. Leland was older and larger than the others.

Two days before Christmas John went to Knoxville. That night when he returned home he had a large package. I was so excited as I was expecting an extremely nice Christmas present. When I opened the package, I found, to my dismay, two pairs of long underwear and two big sticks of peppermint candy. I was so disappointed I could have cried. But, when I started thinking of all the new things we had purchased for our home and about our trip to Middlesboro, I was ashamed of myself. I loved peppermint candy as my father had always bought that for us at Christmas time. I certainly did need the long underwear, for the weather was cold, and we had very little heat in our house.

After Christmas, Mother sent my youngest sister, Dorothy, or Dot, as we called her, to stay with me for a while. She was approximately seven years of age and was such a comfort to me. She attended school in Coal Creek while she was there and was an exceptionally bright student. She liked school very much. She was a healthy looking child, but plump with extremely thick long blond curls hanging almost to her waist. She complained so much of headaches that J.B. decided that the weight of her hair was causing those severe headaches. So, one day he took Dot to the barbershop, and her hair was cut in a nice short bob. This seemed to help her headaches tremendously. She didn't complain so much after that.

She loved to play with the dog someone had given J.B. He was a little white and black fox terrier named "Little J.B." J.B. would put him on the back of the horse and let him ride behind him. However, the dog eventually disappeared, and we thought that someone had probably stolen him as he could entertain you by doing tricks.

One day upon his return from Knoxville, John brought me some beautiful linen. There was enough for me to make a tablecloth and napkins to match. I had never sewn but was able to find a neighbor to help me to cut out the pieces. She also hemmed the napkins and tablecloth for me on her sewing machine.

Sometime that winter, Mother Baldwin came for a visit. She was small, slim, and dainty, and her short hair was white. Everything was all prepared for her arrival. The table was set with the new linen tablecloth and napkins. I had not had much experience with cooking when I married, but that night I had cooked a chicken. I killed the chicken and plucked the black feathers from it. Since I had had difficulty getting all the pin feathers out, I decided to skin the chicken. During dinner that night, Mother Baldwin inquired, "Elizabeth, what became of the skin of this chicken?"

"I had difficulty getting all the pin feathers out, so I skinned it, cleaned it, and then broiled it," I answered.

Mother Baldwin responded, "Never skin a chicken. You're supposed to pluck all the feathers out, and cook it with the skin on it. I'll have to show you how to cook John's favorite foods. These napkins are beautiful but always hem them by hand. You'll have to take all this out and re hem them. I'll help you," she said. Mother Baldwin sewed beautifully and was glad that she could be of assistance.

All that winter we had a man, Ernest, who came every morning to feed the horses. He chopped the wood and brought it in, started the fire in the fireplace, and lit the fire in the coal stove. His wife did my washing except for the doctor's shirts. We always went those to the laundry.

One morning after lighting the fire in the kitchen stove, Ernest knocked on the bedroom door and said, "Doctor, are you up yet?"

J.B. answered, "Yes, we're up."

Ernest inquired with a very frightened look, "There's something on the stove that goes, 'putt-putt, putt-putt.' Is it something that might blow up?"

"Oh, no, Ernest. That's the coffee pot. Mrs. Baldwin fixed that last night, so that it could be ready by the time we got up this morning. Would you like a cup?"

Ernest had never seen a percolator.

One day J.B. received a wire from his sister, Mary, who lived in Riverside, California. She married young and went to California with her husband, Robert Pace. He died shortly after their arrival there. At that time she decided to become a nurse and entered training in Riverside Hospital from which she had just graduated as an RN.

This message was being wired by the conductor of the train that was bringing Mary from Riverside, California, to Knoxville, Tennessee. Mary's wallet was stolen out of her purse while she was in route. Therefore, she had no money to pay for her train ticket. She was asking her brother to please bring enough money with him to pay for her ticket and she would reimburse him later. J.B. met her at the station in Knoxville with the money in his pocket. She always bragged that she rode all the way from California with only a nickel and a penny in her purse.

One night it was foggy and drizzling rain when the doctor was coming across the mountain from a delivery in Briceville around 2:00 A.M. He was riding our bay horse, Dan. Suddenly, a bullet whizzed through the top of the Stetson he was wearing. That was moonshine country and the mountain men must have thought that he was a revenue man. He always thought that he would have been killed if he had not been riding Dan as most of the people he knew would have recognized him.

One night it was raining as we were out in the foot hills that John called "the sticks" when he saw a man coming down the road towards us carrying a long shotgun and a lantern and accompanied by a dog. Although he stopped and scrutinized us critically, he finally continued on his way giving a blood-curdling yell as he passed, leaving us with our feet quaking in our shoes from fear.

The next day a man came to the office and said to J.B., "Doctor, Mrs. Baldwin saved your life last night. You were driving a strange horse and you had a cap on instead of the usual black Stetson you usually wear. Mrs. Baldwin was recognized, so we let you go by. Don't come up in that neighborhood without letting someone know that you're coming." The yell had evidently been a signal to his friends.

One March night John came home about 9:00P.M. As he bent over to kiss me, I felt something warm move inside his overcoat pocket. I said, "What do you have in your pocket?"

He answered, "Reach in there and see what you find."

I reached inside his coat and brought out a tiny red pig just a few hours old. That afternoon as J.B. passed the Black Diamond Mine, a farmer, John Disney, had stopped him to give him a gift for me. The old sow had died and this was the only baby pig she had had. The farmer didn't want to bother with feeding it. At first, we fed him warm milk with a medicine dropper. As she grew larger she learned to drink from a bottle and eventually, she could drink and eat out of a dish like a dog.

Then, a man from Dutch Valley brought us three large geese and one gander. They made themselves at home and built their nest in the back of Dan's stall. Then, a woman from the Better Chance Mine settlement brought me a big brown hen with the chickens just out of the nest. My backyard began to look like a little farm. The doctor sold the half-grown pigs and I made pets out of the chickens. I cried whenever I had to kill one.

John thought that he could put up with my cooking and said that he would try to help me. But, he was critical and laughed at me whenever I made a failure. One warm morning in May, I made some light rolls, but they didn't rise. As I could not throw the dough away without him seeing it, I buried it in the backyard and forgot about it. Later, as John was coming in from the barn for supper, he saw a rise in the ground. He thought it was a mole and went to find a hoe with which he intended to dig it up. However, he dug up my bread instead. The warmth from the sun had caused my bread to rise. It took me a long time to live that one down as he loved to tease me.

When he was a little later than he was expected to be, he told his patients, "My wife made some biscuits, and I gave one to Dan. It slowed him down. I was going to give him a drink of water, but I was afraid that he would swell up."

One morning around 8:00A.M. we were eating breakfast when a loud whistle began to blow. There had been an explosion at one of the mines. The doctor quickly left to see what he could do to help. There were 80 men buried alive none of whom survived the explosion.

In June, 1914, Mary, John's sister called and wanted to borrow Dan to ride to Mammoth Cave. So, J.B. rode Dan over to Middlesboro and rode a big dark bay horse named Frank back.

As soon as school was out for summer vacation, Mother and Daddy and the children moved to Maryville. Leland found a position with Alcoa Aluminum and Jim was also working after school. Polly and Dot came for a visit.

One morning I went out to milk the cow, Suky. Polly was holding the cow's tail so that Suky would not hit me in the face with it as she switched flies while Dot climbed up in the loft to hunt for eggs. As she was searching intently through the loft, she threw an empty basket down. The cow was startled and jumped back, accidently stepping on Polly's toe. Whereupon Polly screamed that her toe was broken. Dot was so frightened that she refused to come down from the loft.

My little red pig was about half-grown by this time, and she had the run of the kitchen. She loved me and followed me everywhere I went. One day while the doctor was operating in his office, Polly and Dot were washing and drying the dishes. At the same time they were playing with the pig. They were flipping their dish cloths at the pig. This made a popping noise and the pig would squeal as she ran around the kitchen and out the door onto the porch. I went out there and said, "If you don't shut up and behave yourselves, the doctor will take care of you after he finishes the operation."

After Polly and Dot went home, J.B. and I went to Middlesboro for a week. While we were there Mother Baldwin took me to the kitchen to teach me how to cook all the things my husband liked. She was a good cook, and when we came back to Coal Creek, I was a good cook, too. My friends came over to see me, and Lee came to spend the weekend. I was sick with a cold, so she helped John in the kitchen.

Upon our return to Coal Creek from Middlesboro, we brought the ten year old son of Mother Baldwin's cook. He name was Abraham Lincoln Alexander, Jr. His mother told John that Abraham was getting out of hand, and she could not manage him. John told her that he would take him home and straighten him out. Abraham was always getting into trouble. He used the doctor's razor to whittle with. This was the only razor J.B. had ever had, and he was partial to it.

July was a busy month with a lot of typhoid and O.B.'s. I went out with him on all O.B.'s. Several times the man who came after the doctor would say, "They told me to bring you if the doctor wasn't there." I would go and help until J.B. could come.

One August morning I had a long distance telephone call from my father. My sister, Polly, was extremely ill, and he wanted me to come to see her right away. Another doctor was treating her but she wasn't improving any. I went over on the morning train, and Daddy met me at the station. She was critically ill and had all the symptoms of typhoid. Her temperature was 105, and I felt very frightened as many typhoid cases were dying. I called John and he said to put her on a cot and bring her home on the morning train. Just talking to him over the phone seemed to have a calming effect on me. I immediately began to pack a few things that Polly and Dot would need during their stay, and Daddy drove us to the station. We were put in the baggage compartment. Dot and I stayed right with Polly.

When we returned home, we put her cot in our room. Off and on she would lose consciousness. J.B. examined her and then we put ice caps on her head. As we could not get her temperature down, J. B. called the barber to come over and shave her head. Her hair was matted and difficult to comb. While shaving Polly's head, the barber was careful to preserve her long curls in a cap like form so that they could be fitted back on just in case we were not able to pull her through the long drawn out illness we were facing. When the barber had finished, it was easier to keep ice packs on her.

J. B. told me that I could not take care of Polly and do the cooking, too, as typhoid was very contagious. Of course, we did not want the food to be contaminated. So, I called Mother and asked her if she would come over to do the cooking. She came on the next train.

Finally, in September, Polly was better and well enough to be up and around. We were all so relieved and pleased with her progress toward recovery. Mother went home, but Dot stayed and attended school in Coal Creek. As Polly began to get better she became cross and refused to take her medicine. J. B. promised her that she could have the German Shepherd puppy someone had given him, if she would only take her medicine. She finally agreed to this. When she was well enough to go home, J.B. put both Polly and Dot on the train for Maryville. He also sent Abraham Lincoln Alexander, Jr. to Middlesboro.

Just about the time I was getting my little four room house to look like a real home, John rented the large red wooden house across the street. It had four rooms and a hall downstairs and four bedrooms upstairs. Our little bit of furniture would not have been enough to fill two of those large rooms; therefore, the doctor made a trip to Knoxville where he bought a rug, bed, and dresser for our room and furniture for the dining room. He bought nice heavy walnut furniture that would last a hundred years. Then, he bought several hospital beds from the hospital that had closed down before we were married. I dyed my white curtains yellow with tea as I wanted them to match my golden wedding ring.

John rented two of the bedrooms to teachers. He rented one room to a Miss Cos and the other to a Mr. and Mrs. Foster. They paid me $12.50 a month for room and breakfast. My sisters, Charlotte and Dot came over for a while. Charlotte was a great help to me.

The doctor came home one afternoon and said to me, "Miss Cox would like to borrow your riding skirt."

I said, "Why?"

"She is going to ride Dan this afternoon," he answered.

I said, "Why didn't she ask me?"

He laughed. When Miss Cox came home from school, she came to get my skirt. While she was changing, I went out to talk to Dan. I pulled his ear down close to my mouth and said to him, "Don't take Miss Cox any further than the creek. You may go get a big drink and then come right back."

Dan always loved to go into the deep water to get a long drink. The doctor helped Miss Cox mount Dan and then she rode off. In a little while she returned.

I said, "Why did you come back?"

She answered, "I couldn't get him to go any further than the creek. He took a long drink and then turned around and started towards home. I couldn't make him go any farther."

After Miss Cox went inside the house, I petted Dan and gave him some sugar. That night J.B. said, "I wonder what is wrong with Dan this afternoon. That wasn't like him."

I said, "I told him to come home." He laughed.

On the 8th of October, which was on a Sunday, Bunny came over from Middlesboro and spent the day. He was not feeling well. An old woman had told him that vinegar would help him to reduce. He always took his lunch to work: So one day he bought a jar of pickles. He ate all of the pickles for lunch and then drank all of the vinegar which was in the jar. He had felt much worse ever since that day. J.B. examined him and gave him some medicine.

I cooked a chicken for dinner. When J.B. started to carve it, it slipped off the plate and landed in his lap. I laughed and he became angry. As Charlotte, Dot, and I could not stop laughing, we had to leave the table to appease his anger.

It was a lovely fall day, and we made some photographs. Bunny had to leave on the afternoon train, as he had to go to work the next day.

On the morning of November 14, 1914, around 8:00A.M. I had a telephone call from Lee. She said that another former roommate of ours, Mary Lou Pendergrass, whom we called Pendy, and Bob Taylor, a young lawyer and a close friend of ours, were getting married in the First Baptist Church in Knoxville at 12:00 noon. It would be a double wedding as Lee and Clyde Peake were also being married at that time. She wanted us to catch the 10:00 A.M. train to Knoxville. She also requested that John stop off at the Court House to buy the license for both couples.

John had gone to the post office. I called him, and we caught the train. Carolyn Volena Lee and Clyde Peake and Pendy and Bob Taylor were married at 12:00 Noon. John was Bob's best man. When he handed the ring to Bob, he dropped it, and it rolled all the way across the floor. Harrison's boy friend, Hugh, was Clyde's best man.

Afterwards, they were all standing around talking, John said, "Well, we will have to be going as I have some calls to make when we get back. Why don't you come home with us (I don't think he meant it?)

Someone replied, "Fine, do you really mean it?"

"Of course," he said, "Come on." They came home with us, Lee, Clyde, Pendy, and Bob. No one will ever know how I felt. I had never cooked for anyone except John, Dot, Polly, and Abraham. Charlotte did most of the cooking when she was with me. I knew that we did not have enough food in the house for all those hungry men. Clyde Peake was a big man who loved to eat, and Bob Taylor was always hungry.

When we returned to Coal Creek, John went to the grocery store to buy the food for the week-end. Lee and Pendy helped me prepare supper. Then, I made up my bed downstairs for Lee and Clyde. I made up two of the hospital beds upstairs, which I pushed together, for Pendy and Bob. We all had a nice visit. After breakfast they caught the 10:00 A.M. train back to Knoxville. It all seemed like a dream.

The rest of November was cold and wet. John had a lot of country calls to make and caught a bad cold. The night before he had been out in the rain most of the night. Dr. Dixon came to see him and took care of his patients. I went to see the ones that were bedridden, and I also went with Dr. Dixon on O.B.'s when he needed me.

John was in bed about a week. It was hard to keep him in as long as Dr. Dixon would have liked him to stay in. My phone and doorbell rang at all hours of the day and night. The patients would say, "They told me if the doctor was not able to come to bring his wife."

About the middle of December, John had a call from his mother saying that Bunny was extremely ill. She wanted John to come to see him. He went to Middlesboro and brought Bunny home with him. On Monday he took him to Knoxville to see a kidney specialist. When they returned, I could tell that John was distressed. About a week later, we took Bunny and went to Middlesboro for Christmas. It was not a Merry Christmas as Bunny was in bed most of the time.

We went back to Coal Creek two days after Christmas. We brought Bunny with us as John refused to leave him. He grew steadily worse each day and died in convulsions on January 5, 1915.

The next few days were hard on my husband. He and Bunny had been close and he was deeply aggrieved by our lose. J.B. had all the arrangements to make, telephone calls and a wire to the family that lived in Arkansas. Rodney was in Middlesboro with Mother Baldwin. Mary was in New Mexico. The office was closed. Dr. Dixon took care of our patients. Ernest always took care of the livestock while we were away. I had to sell Suky and my little red pig to the butcher. Mr. Findley, the butcher, came to my back door and said, "Mrs. Baldwin, I can't get your little red pig to cross the bridge. Would you come out and lead him across the bridge to the butcher shop, please?"

That was the hardest thing I had to do. I loved all my pets; but I said, "Come on my little red pie." She followed me all the way across the bridge to the butcher's shop, and I cried all the way. I hated to sell my pets, but John said that we didn't know when we would be back. He didn't want to impose on someone to take care of the livestock for an extended period of time. If Ernest would take care of Dan, we would sell all the other animals. It was very cold weather and rainy. Ice covered everything.

John and I took the body to Nicholasville, Kentucky, to be buried in the family plot at the cemetery. We had to go to Knoxville to change trains to Nicholasville. Rodney and his mother were already there waiting for us. After the funeral we went home with Aunt Ella Flynn, who was John's father's sister. She lived in Winchester. We were there two days visiting old friends and relatives.

When we returned to Coal Creek, I missed my livestock as I petted them all. John was not well. He had not regained the weight he had lost after having pneumonia the previous Fall. The calls were many, and I went with him all the time now.

February was a wet, cold month, and there were many sick babies and O.B.'s. John was still not feeling well. Around the middle of the month, he went to Knoxville to see Dr. Lumas. They were friends. John thought that if Dr. Lumas could not tell him what the problem was, he could send him to a doctor that could help him. He was gone three days. Dr. Lumas sent him to the hospital for x-rays and a thorough examination.

When he came home, John was depressed and discouraged. The doctor had told him that he would have to stop work and try to build himself up. He was advised to go to Denver, Colorado, to see a Dr. Perkins, who had been having success in cases like his. John's brother, Nat, had moved from Arkansas to Colorado and now lived sixteen miles North of Denver. Nat was now running a big wheat ranch for his father-in-law, Mr. Andrew Johnson. John thought that this would be a nice place to go first.

I wanted him to go immediately and by train. But, he said that Dr. Lumas had told him that no doctor would operate on him until he had gained 10-15 lbs. The most he had ever weighed was 175 lbs, but he now had lost down to 140 lbs. I tried to give him all the nourishing foods I could.

The next two months were busy ones. Rodney came over to help get things started. He made a small sheet iron box with a lid. The lid was separate so that I could take it off and that made it easier to pack supplies in.

We decided to make the trip in our open Studebaker, hug-me-tight buggy in order to get as much of the sunlight and open air as possible. To pull the buggy we took our Kentucky thoroughbred, Dan, who was the great grandson of the famous racehorse, Dan Patch. Dan Patch won the Kentucky Derby for harness racing in 1903. For supplies we had about a dozen cans the size of a one pound coffee can for such items as coffee, sugar, flour, grits, lard, and other necessities. The piece of reinforced sheet iron which Rodney had made was used as a container for the supplies. A 7 x 7 tent and two camp cots or army cots were secured from Sears & Roebuck. A trench in which a fire was built, was dug out of the ground and a rack placed over it so that a coffee pot, frying pan, or other utensils could be placed thereon. The cots were slipped into an appliance underneath the bed of the buggy where they would be out of the way, and a box of food was placed in the back. On top of this box were stored the pillow and blankets, and above all was placed the tent as it was waterproof and would protect the remainder of our necessities. Afterward the tent poles were strapped to the sides of the buggy, and all was then tied securely in place. Dan's food, 100 lbs. of oats, was placed in front of the buggy, and dresses and extra trousers were carried in the box under the buggy seat. A little black Gladstone bag held all our toilet articles, shaving supplies, and personal belongings.

Everything that I wanted to save was packed into my large trunk and several boxes, including the doctor's books, instruments, and all of our clothes except for two suits of everyday things and one suit for Sunday. I had two middy suits made of cotton and three sets of underwear. John had three tan cotton shirts and two pairs of light weight pants as well as his best black suit. I also took one dark blue suit.

The last ten days of April my father came over to help with the auction and packing. He was planning to take my trunk and other things that we didn't want to sell home with him. As soon as school was out for the summer, Mother and Daddy were planning to move the family back to Greenlee, N.C.

Lee
Nancy Morton

Elizabeth was in nurse's training

Home of Dr. Baldwin

Nancy Morton

Nancy Morton

Nancy Morton

Nancy Morton

Grandfather Baldwin

Grandmother Greenlee & Elizabeth

Studebaker-Hug-me-tight buggy
Dan the horse

Grandfather Baldwin

Aunt Mary Casey

The Honeymoon

On the third of May, a beautiful sunshiny day, the men came to sell my beloved things. My father understood how I felt. I went out on the side porch where I could not see anyone and had a good long cry. I would never see my beautiful antique lamp or my cut glass dishes again. They were given to me for wedding presents, and I prize them very much. I could hear the auctioneer's voice in the background as my lovely possessions were going one by one. It was heartbreaking. By noon everything was sold. The boxes and trunk were at the depot to go home with Daddy. The train left at 3:00P.M. Then, we packed the buggy. Rodney had taught me to unpack the tent and put it up. I had to practice about six times before I was able to get it to stay. I had to learn to do this as John was not strong enough. The metal food box was put in first. Beside it went a butcher knife, flying pan, coffee pot, large fork, and cake turner. We also took a small saucepan, two cups, two plates, as well as several knives, forks, and spoons. At 6:00P.M. I had my last look at the home where I had been so happy for 15 months. John shook hands with the people who had come to see us off, and Rodney kissed me goodbye. We were off. By 10:00 P.M. we were in LaFollette, Tennessee, where we spent the night at the LaFollette Hotel.

At 6:00A.M. Tuesday, May 4, 1915, we had breakfast at the hotel and started on our long journey which was destined to be even longer and more arduous than either of us could have anticipated. I wanted to go, and would have never allowed him to go alone. However, I had never slept outside in my live, and I was frightened. I silently prayed all day. I knew that we did not have enough money to stay in hotels, and I knew that John would be unhappy if he knew I was afraid. So, I just kept on praying and pretended to enjoy every minute. It was a beautiful day and Dan looked so pretty. We stopped at 12:00 Noon and ate a delicious lunch which the hotel had prepared for us. Dan was fed and watered at a small creek nearby.

We crossed out of Tennessee by the Cumberland Gap, and around 7:00P.M. we made camp right outside of Middlesboro, Kentucky. My heart was up in my throat by that time. I was going to have to put the tent up by myself for the first time as John was too weak to do it. He made the fire and began to prepare our dinner while I unhitched Dan and fed him. Then, I started on the tent. It fell down several times, and I mashed my thumb. But, I had it up and our cots made up by the time John had supper ready. By that time it was dark. We lit the lantern and hung it on the middle tent pole. Of course, I was expecting a snake or a spider, but I only saw a baby rabbit.

The next morning we were up at daylight. I fed and watered Dan, took the tent down, and packed the buggy while John cooked breakfast. After we had eaten, I went across the road and brought my second bucket of water from a well in a churchyard. Then, I proceeded to wash the dishes. John heated some water in the coffeepot to be used for shaving. I pulled out a small mirror which he hung on the side of a tree.

By 7:00A.M. we were on our way. It was all new country for me, and I had heard some stories about how lawless the Eastern Kentucky people were. But, the day was nice and at noon we stopped at a grocery store where we bought some cheese, crackers, and beer. By about 5:00 or 6:00 P.M., a thunderstorm was brewing. Before the rain began, we met a farmer, a Mr. Jackson, who allowed us to drive into his barn for shelter. John told him who he was. He turned out to be a good friend of my brother-in-law, Bunny. Mr. Jackson insisted on us having supper with him and his wife and also invited us to spend the night. We accepted his invitation for dinner, but John did not want to impose upon his generosity any further. So, when the storm ended, we thanked him for the delicious dinner and continued on our way. We traveled late. Upon our arrival in Barbourville, we went to the hotel as the ground was too wet for camping.

We had a nice restful night and a good breakfast. I was so glad that it had rained. John and I both felt better, and I am sure that Dan did, too. We were getting up in the "sticks" that I would have called the foot hills where John had said was noted for its moonshiners. That night, May 6, we camped on the outskirts of London.

After breakfast the next morning, we stopped at a grocery store to refill our supplies as my small one pound cans did not last very long. We had reached the Laurel Country, a remote and lawless section in the mountains of Kentucky that is also known as the moonshine country where family feuding still existed at the time. Also, in this section there is what is known as the Big Hill, an incline which ascends gradually but continuously for fourteen miles to the summit. Then, at that point begins a precipitous descent down for about a mile to the foot of the hill. The night following we were able to camp at the foot of the hill as it was the only level place large enough for the tent.

The next morning John was in good spirits. He said, "We are in God's country, now." All morning we passed large white houses with white fences and beautiful horses. We proceeded on to Richmond, Kentucky, where we had dinner. That afternoon we crossed the Kentucky River by pull ferry at Valley View. Dan did not seem afraid to go on, but I was frightened. While we were crossing the river, my beautiful white panama hat, which I had bought to protect my face from the sun, blew off into the swiftly moving river. As it floated downstream, J.B. looked at me and said, "Please don't cry. We'll buy another" but we never did. We camped early that night near its banks as we were both tired.

We were up early the next morning and in Nicholasville by 10:00 A.M., where we proceeded to Aunt Mary Barkley's as that was where Mother Baldwin was. Aunt Mary and Mother Baldwin were sisters. After Bunny died, Mother Baldwin had moved back here from Middlesboro. After greeting everyone, we had nice hot baths and dinner. Aunt Mary's cook, Aunt Lu, had prepared all of John's favorite foods.

After dinner we went out to the Baldwin home and met Mrs. Jacobs, who had bought the place from Mother Baldwin. But, Mother Baldwin had never sold the pasture which was across the street. It has a tall metal fence all around it. There we stayed for two weeks, camping in his mother's pasture in order to become accustomed to this kind of life before really starting on our long journey westward. During this time John boarded Dan at the livery stable where he could be taken care of and fed regularly.

Then, we went visiting. John had lots of friends, and we were invited out every night by either family or friends. We were surrounded by them during the daytime as well. We spent one night in Winchester with Aunt Ella and Uncle Louis Flynn. He also took me to Lexington. We had two wonderful weeks.

One morning John went to the livery stable to see Dan, and when he returned, he had a tiny fox terrier puppy about six weeks old. He was white with a black spot on is back and one black ea. He named him Jerd after the old man who had given him the puppy.

Aunt Lu prepared us enough food to last several days. After packing the buggy we went inside to tell Aunt Mar, Mother Baldwin, and Aunt Lu goodbye whereupon we continued on our way to Frankfort, Kentucky. When I packed the bedclothes, I left one pillow on top for the puppy. John said, "That's your pillow, not mine." The pup slept in my lap part of the time. When he became restless, John could let us walk a little way. When we were back in the buggy, I would put him on the pillow back of my head. We did not have dog food, so I fed him scraps of our food and canned milk.

We arrived in Frankfort around 5:00P.M. Where one of my husband's friends was warden of the Federal Prison. He insisted on our coming out to the prison and having dinner with him. He had a private dining room, and the only prisoners we saw were long lines of men going in for their dinner. We left around sundown and camped outside of Frankfort.

On May 25, we arose at daylight. John prepared breakfast as usual while I fed and watered Dan and took the tent down. By that time, I thought I was an expert camper. I could have the tent down and folded by the time John called me to breakfast. He had to shave, and by 7:30A.M. we were on our way.

That night we camped outside of Shelbyville, near Louisville. This section of Kentucky is noted for its beautiful bluegrass and thoroughbred race horses. After setting up camp, I went to a nearby house to ask for water. An old lady came to the door. Upon my request for water, she informed me, "We have no water for tramps!" whereupon she slammed the door in my face. I continued on to the next house where the woman obligingly gave me all the water I needed.

The next morning I said to John, "I hope that you'll go get the water this morning." Well, he took the bucket and went to the third house and rang the doorbell. He was gone so long that I was beginning to worry. Then, I looked up and saw him coming across the road loaded down with food including hot biscuits, fresh strawberries, strawberry jam, fresh cream, and other good things to eat as well.

When he rang the doorbell, a woman had come to the door and said, "Why, John Baldwin, what are you doing here? Come in and have breakfast with me." She was an old sweetheart of his from his teenage years. We had a delightful breakfast that morning and were late getting started.

At Louisville, Kentucky, we crossed the Ohio River at a toll bridge where the fee was 35 cents. We continued on to New Albany, Indiana, where we camped for the night outside of town. I managed to put the tent up and feed and water Dan before the hard rain came. This was my first hard thunderstorm out –of-doors. Fortunately, we still had food from Aunt Lu's basket, and the tent kept us dry.

The next morning was cloudy and drizzling. I fed and watered Dan and packed the buggy. John said, "We will not try to prepare our breakfast this morning as everything is too wet." We continued on into New Albany where we had breakfast at the hotel. It was an old-fashioned hotel with the most beautiful antique furniture. After breakfast it was still raining hard, so we spent the day at the hotel. Both of us had a welcome bath, and we sent our clothes to the laundry. John looked at the map and decided how far we could travel in a week's time. Then, he paid the proprietor of the laundry for serving our clothes as well as postage to French Lick which was the next large town. When we went through French Lick, we would go to the post office and claim our laundry. I enjoyed every minute of this rain.

The next day was Friday, May 28, 1915. It was still cloudy and cold, but we started out about 7:30 A.M. after a good breakfast. At noon it was still drizzling. Being forced to wear a sweater or light coat in order to keep warm, we soon came to a cross-road saloon. In those days, women were not allowed to go into saloons. John stopped the buggy and went in to inquire as to whether his wife could come in out of the rain. The bar tender said, "Of course," whereupon we went in and seated ourselves as inconspicuously as possible. We ordered sandwiches and two mugs of draught beer. We proceeded to warm ourselves thoroughly. John had told me before we were married, "I like a drink every now and then. I also smoke, and I like to play poker. I want a wife that can do all of the things I do as she's going to be my companion all of my life. If you cannot learn to do all the things I do, I'll go out and find someone who can." Therefore, I did learn to do all those things. We stayed at the cross-road saloon until it stopped raining, and then, we continued on our way.

That night it was still sprinkling rain and as everything was wet, we stopped at a hotel in a little town called Paoli. We had another night inside with baths and wonderful meals.

When we started out the next morning, the sun was shining, and we were rested. Dan had spent the night in a livery stable and looked so good. We made good time. So, about 5:30P.M. we stopped for the night a few miles from a big gambling town, French Lick, Indiana. Widely known as a health resort for hot baths, it was best known for a mineral which bubbled up out of the ground called Pluto Water. It tasted like Epsom Salts and was sold by the glass over the counter at fountains, necessitating a row of baths nearby. From the music and noise coming from it, there must have been dancing for the patients.

John prepared supper. There was no difficulty finding water as there was a little creek insight. However, the music from the springs played very loudly until way after Midnight and that made it difficult to sleep.

Sunday morning dawned bright and beautiful. I did some washing in the White River. The water's edge was very shallow and clear. When, suddenly. My wedding ring came off. I calmly felt all around in the sand and small multi-colored pebbles until I finally retrieved it. I finished my wash and hung the clothes on the nearby bush to dry. As my wedding ring was too large for my fingers, I asked John to please wear it so that I wouldn't lose it again. We had a nice restful day with no noise from the hot springs. John fished some, and I played with the puppy. He was growing so fast and would retrieve things to me whenever I threw them.

We awoke to a lovely day, warm and sunny and began our regular morning chores. After I packed the buggy, John had to tie the rope securely around the tent as I could not fasten it tightly enough to stay.

Around noontime we stopped at a little grocery store where we bought some cheese crackers, and sardines. John took he bucket and had it filled with draught beer as it held about a quart. We always stopped around the same time every day so that Dan could rest and have lunch. We ate while he did, and the pup learned to eat the things we did.

That night we camped near Lawrenceville, and John went into town to buy supplies for our one pound cans. He also bought a newspaper, cigarettes, T-bone steak, and peppermint stick candy as he knew how much I loved candy. The steak was a special treat for us, and after supper, Jerd went out and buried the bone. We had been traveling about a month, and I still was not accustomed to sleeping out-of–doors.

As we proceeded on our trip, I admired the beautiful country side of Indiana and Illinois as it was similar to the country around Nicholasville, Kentucky. Most of the time John felt good, but as the days became warmer, he had to rest longer at noon. We also began to stop earlier in the evening. His appetite remained good, but he had very little strength.

We crossed out of Indiana by the Wabash River at Vincennes. Soon began a week of cold rain all through Illinois. During this period the nights were spent in hotels. Several days were spent in a very old historic hotel which was furnished completely with beautiful antique furniture. The proprietor of the hotel did not object to the pup as he was completely trained and well-behaved. We soon found our financial resources to be at a very low ebb.

We proceeded on to East St. Louis where we crossed the Mississippi River by the Eads Bridge, on the middle of which a little pay station for the toll bridge was located. The fee was 35cents. It was around 4:00P.M., and our money was completely gone. John put Dan in a livery stable, and I went to the telegraph office where I pawned my wedding ring for enough money to send a telegram to Mother Baldwin. We then went to a cheap second-rate hotel, the Holland House at St. Louis, Missouri, where John put his watch up as collateral for room and board. We then had to wait until more money could reach us from Mother Baldwin through general delivery. We had six uncomfortable days before the money came. About all we could do was window shop, and that we did to our heart's content.

When the money finally came, we packed and prepared to leave St. Louis. John paid the hotel bill, but the manager refused to return his gold watch. After some cursing and swearing on John's part, the man finally relinquished his watch.

I went to the telegraph office to retrieve my ring. Then, we bought groceries, supplies, and feed for Dan. We left St. Louis early on the morning of June 12. The day before had been my birthday, and I was 26 years old. We started out early and made good mileage as Dan was well rested. The man at the livery stable had told John of an old road that was part of the Santa Fe Trail. It was a good road and better for the horse's feet. It kept us away from the automobiles, and we by-passed the big cities.

The weather was good, but dry, dusty, and sandy. The grass was parched and would have been quick to catch fire. I remembered that Mother Baldwin had told me to watch for a blue jay on Friday. The legend states that they all go to Hell to carry brimstone to the Devil on Friday. So, I began to watch for blue jays every day of the week. We crossed the Charles River for 50 cents and found a nice camping spot.

I continuously watched the sky for signs of storms as many people had told me that it was storm time in Missouri. John said, "You are wearing the knees out of your hose praying to Heaven that the weather will stay clear of storms."

Upon our arrival in Odessa, Missouri, J.B. and I went to a post office where a box containing a large fruitcake, beaten biscuits, and a baked ham was waiting for us along with other things. We picked up our laundry which had been mailed from the last town we had visited. After securing feed for Dan, we went back out into the country to find a camping spot, and we soon came to a ranch house where we asked permission to camp. We were directed to a fenced-in pasture where we proceeded to set up camp; and since John wanted to go back to town, I went with him as he did not want me to stay alone.

Several hours later we returned to find our tent flattened, most of our food gone, and an old sow in the middle of my cot with all four legs down through the canvas squealing like mad.

That night we had a terrible storm with winds so high that it blew the buggy up against the fence. So, the next morning J.B. informed me that we were going into town and sell Dan. I said, "No, you're not going to sell Dan!"

"I am not going to have you crying every time you see a cloud in the sky," said J.B.

"Well, I'll try not to think about the storms any more, but I simply couldn't bear to sell Dan," whereupon he agreed not to sell him. Then, I went out and hugged Dan and gave him an apple. I told him that we would never sell him.

Between Kansas City and Independence, Missouri, we came upon an old enormous castle-like house surrounded by a large brick wall. The house was vacant, but the care-taker gave us permission to camp inside the wall. We decided to go into Kansas City, where we found a nice restaurant and had a good supper. It was so good to put our feet under a table again.

Finally, we returned to camp to find our tent again on the ground. Too, it was raining and lightning, and the thunder was foreboding a terrible storm. Dan would not answer our call, and since his food was all that seemed to be missing this time, we surmised that it was he who had done all the damage. I had forgotten to feed him before we left. Evidently, he had smelled his food inside the tent, and tried to get it for himself. In this attempt, he had knocked the tent down. We were camped underneath a tree, and I was so frightened all night that I could not sleep.

The next day we began out trip through Kansas, 700 miles. The weather remained hot, dry, and sunny during the daytime with terrible storms at night. We had passed through Kansas City and had stopped to eat lunch. We did not usually build a fire at noontime as we did not want to take that much time. I lit our sterno stove upon which I boiled some eggs, and then I prepared some sandwiches. The banks which rose from each side of the road appeared to be just high enough to make a good place to rest. John went across the road and sat down to rest upon what he thought to be an old dead log. He quickly arose and when he turned around, I could see that his backside was full of spines from the large cactus bush upon which he had accidentally sat. He said, "Please come here and help me." Cars continued to pass, blowing their horns and people were waving to us. The spines from the cactus were white against his black broadcloth trousers.

Probably the most trying time which we experienced took place several days later at Olathe, Kansas. There was a storm nearly every night during this part of our journey, but on this occasion there was a particularly vicious one which almost assumed the proportions of a tornado. Soon after we camped, the wind began to race constantly until it seemed that nothing could stand against it, and along with the heavy rain that accompanied it assumed very dangerous proportions. The wind blew over a bucket of water sitting on the ground, blew the buggy against a high fence, and the water rushed under us across the floor of the tent in torrents. Our sterno stove which was sitting on the cot was blown over catching it on fire. I immediately picked up my Blue Book and put out the fire. A Blue Book is a traveler's guide which informs its readers of good hotels, restaurants, and camping spots all across the country. It even had blank pages in the back which I had been using for a diary. We were literally frightened out of our wits. Even a mirror which was fastened to the tent pole was completely soaked and melted out of its frame. In addition every little while we had to go out again and drive the stakes in deeper to secure the tent to its moorings. However, this terrible night finally passed, and the following day dawned bright and beautiful.

As I was currying Dan, John came up to me and said, "Babe, curry him well, and we'll take him into town and sell him. I'm not going to have you crying and being frightened to death this way again. We shall finish the trip by train."

But, I told him that since we had come this far we were not going to change our mode of travel now. Selling Dan was not mentioned again, and we continued on our way.

I was sitting in the buggy the next night just as it was getting dark. John was in a butcher shop when a traveler came by and noticed the mason pin which I was wearing. He turned out to be a man who lived in the immediate vicinity and asked if he could be of any help to us. If so, we had only to let him know. However, he furnished us with a nice camping spot on his land. As there was a very threatening black cloud in the sky, we hurried to get the tent up and succeeded in doing so just before the storm struck.

A day or two later when we were passing through some beautiful rolling country, we came to a beautiful little creek which was lined with willows, and the road crossed it by means of a picturesque wooden bridge with no railing. John said, I believe I shall stop and fish for a while. It is such a beautiful place." I decided to drive on since I had no desire to sit there and watch him fish. Leaving him there, I drove on up the road, but after only a few minutes I rounded a curve and was faced with a very large and attractive white house on the porch of which sat a lady stringing beans. When she saw me she immediately said, "Come on up here and rest for a while. Would you like something to drink?"

I answered, "Oh, yes, I would." I climbed down from the buggy, crossed the lawn, climbed up the steps, sat down beside her, and began helping her to string beans. I explained that my husband was fishing and that I had wanted to get out of the sun.

After a while my husband came across the lawn carrying his fishing pole but no fish. He came up on the porch whereupon he was offered something cool to drink. The woman and her husband were very hospitable and invited us for supper whereupon we accepted with gratitude. We had a delicious home cooked country dinner with homemade biscuits, ham, and vegetables.

They wanted us to spend the night, so J.B. suggested that we put our tent up in the front yard next to the rock wall. However, they did permit us to take a much welcomed bath.

When we awoke the next morning, the lady of the household had our breakfast all prepared. We ate a big country breakfast. She had the best light bread and gave me some starter in a little jar with which we could make pancakes.

The rainy weather, however, continued, and every time we left our tent, we returned to find it flattened by pigs or cattle. Rolling and attractive, this section of Eastern Kansas was beautiful, camping spots were nice, and fishing was good.

The mosquitos were terrible, so J.B. bought a mesh netting which completely covered Dan and protected him from the mosquitos. He also bought a straw hat and cut one hole on each side so that his ears could go through. This also protected his eyes from the sunlight. Another method of protection against the mosquitos which we used was to burn rags and paper inside the tent at night. My poor little puppy was bitten, too.

Later, at Huchinson, Kansas, we went into town and were unable to find a camping place. Consequently, John went to the mayor and showed his Elk card. We were then allowed to camp in the park across from which a carnival was going full blast. John went across the street to investigate. When he returned he said that he had a proposition for me. The owner of the carnival had told him that his gypsy was ill. His offer was to braid my hair, come over to the carnival and use their gypsy tent for telling fortunes. Finally, I was to have all the money that I made. Never the less I told him we didn't need the money. John thought that it was a great joke and teased me about if continuously thereafter..

It was not all one-sided, however, for not long after this when we were at a circus, he was persuaded to dance with the circus midget. The circus owners even tried their best to convince John to join the circus and go with them, because the act had turned out to really be a riot. Originally, he had intended it only as a joke.

As we progressed through middle Kansas there were no large towns, and the only one of any size was Dodge City, where we remained for six days due to the fact that once again our money was completely exhausted. To send a wire by Western Union, John had to give his watch and cuff links and I my wedding ring as security. We went to The Dodge House, a second-rate hotel again to wait for our money to catch up with us.

Finally, when our money came and we went back to pay our bills and to rescue our belongings, the Dodge House manager did not want to return John's watch, but after some cussing he finally agreed to do so.

Moving then into Western Kansas, we found the country to be quite the opposite of Eastern Kansas in most respects. Many of the people were Germans who refused us camping sites and were generally uncooperative in every way. One morning while in this area I awoke to find a rattlesnake curled up underneath my cot. J.B. quickly pulled out his pistol and killed it.

For the past several days, Dan had been ill which we attributed to the alfalfa he had accidentally eaten and the alkali water which he drank from a mud puddle after a hard storm. Alkali water has a peculiar taste and acts just like a dose of salts. From then on we watched Dan more carefully to see that he did not eat or drink anything which would continue to make him ill. It was difficult to buy oats while in this vicinity, so we substituted corn. As this alkali water would have also made J.B. ill, I always had to taste it before I gave it to either of them to drink. If the water tasted terrible, I knew that it was not good to drink. At one time while we were in this vicinity we found that there was a scarcity of water. I managed to purchase about a quart for 25 cents, but when I started to give some of it to Dan, the woman became angry saying that it was not for horses.

Just after we crossed the boundary line into Colorado, J.B. said, "Now, we'll just have to stop, for Dan's sake. He just can't go any farther until he is better." We were able to rent an empty house near Holly to give Dan better care and some rest as well. We pitched our tent on the front lawn. There was a tree under which Dan could stay in the daytime to keep out of the hot sun. There we remained for a week or ten days and doctored him with oat meal, raw eggs, paregoric, and bismuth. After this rest and treatment, Dan was better and we decided to resume our journey.

Soon we passed through a ghost town which had been a fair-sized town. However, now there was not a living thing there. The sidewalks, stores, hotels, and other establishments were still there. Evidently, this had been a railroad town. When that particular section of the railroad was completed, everyone had moved away.

At this time we were entering the cantaloupe, honey dew melon, and sugar beet country, and after passing through Pueblo, we proceeded on to Colorado Springs, where we had to have the buggy fixed. Not wishing to watch this tiresome job, I decided to go to the dime store for a while where John agreed to pick me up when the buggy was ready. I was wearing a brown middy suit and a brown cloth hat made of poplin material. The hair pins in my hair had worn holes through the hat allowing my hair to come up through the holes.

While I was standing in front of the store waiting, two cowboys came by and said, "Humph! I didn't know that there was a carnival in town." I was sunburned to such an extent that they evidently believed me to be a gypsy.

From there on into Denver, we were warned not to pitch camp in low places or under power lines for storms came up very suddenly, and in the arroyas or dry water beds the water rises so swiftly in such places that everything could be washed away or people could even drown at any time during the day or night. For the remainder of the trip to Denver, we were especially careful where we camped because of this warning. When we did camp we did so only on the highest ground to be found in the vicinity.

One Sunday afternoon around 3:00 P.M. we passed a wagon load of boys and girls who were evidently on a hay ride. As we drove past, on boy shouted to another, "Oh, look at the gypsies!"

J.B. laughed and said, "Go back and beat them up."

On the morning of August 4, 1915, the day we rode into Denver, J.B. shot a dove. I picked it clean and cooked it over the sterno stove. As we were eating, J.B. looked at me and said, "Well, we're almost to Denver. Our trip is nearly over. Are you glad?"

I answered, "No, I'd just soon continue."

That afternoon, three long months after leaving Coal Creek, Tennessee, we rode into Denver where we studied the map to decide which road to take to get out to Broomfield. Broomfield was only a crossroad and sixteen miles from Denver. We asked directions and arrived at Nat's house in time for supper. I was very impressed with Denver, and I thought that it was the most beautiful city I had ever seen. Even throughout the summer, the snowcapped mountains lend a picturesque look to the city.

Roomfield

Nat's father-in-law, Mr. J. Andrew Johnson, had rented a large wheat farm which he and his two son-in-laws' ran. J.B. and I drove up in front of an average-sized white cottage surrounded by several cottonwood trees. Approximately fifty feet from the house was a large pond. In the winter when the pond was frozen over, Nat would cut large blocks of ice which would be taken to their ice house located not too far away from the pond. The ice was then covered with straw which helped to prevent it from melting.

Nat also had lots of chickens, hogs, a few cows, and other farm animals. The Johnsons, Mamie's sister, Eunice, and her husband, Henry, lived not very far from each other.

There we received a very warm welcome from everyone. Mama Johnson had prepared a delicious dinner at her house for us, and after dinner the men talked for hours. I was so exhausted that I fell asleep sitting up. Mamie was short and stout with beautiful fair complexion and long dark hair. She had a lovely personality and made us feel welcome for the two months that we were guests in her home. During this time, John and I rested from our trip, I helped Mamie with the household chores while John visited his doctor and tried to build himself up in preparation for his operation.

One pretty sunshiny afternoon, Mamie and I went for a ride in the buggy. As I was driving the horse, three of the prettiest little kittens ran across the road in front of us. They were black with white streaks down their backs. Suddenly Mamie said, "Oh! Stop quick! What pretty kittens. I want one of those. I'm going to try to catch one of them."

I said, "Oh, no. Let's not catch them. They're out of sight now any way."

That night at the supper table, I told Nat of our afternoon excursion. He laughed, clapped his hands together, and said, "I wish to God that she had caught it.

But, one day poor little Jerd did catch one and had to be washed and put up in the barn until the smell subsided.

Nat was approximately six feet tall with average weight, brown hair and twinkly eyes. He loved people and enjoyed talking about when he and his brother were children and the jokes they played on each other.

He had previously worked as an engineer for the railroad until his eye-sight failed. Then, he went to work for his father-in-law.

Mr. Johnson had a big beautiful automobile, a white steamer, which Nat borrowed to drive us around Denver and show us the sights.

Denver

We stayed with Mamie and Nat until October when we were able to rent a one-room apartment with a bath in Denver for $13.00 per month. It had a sink, hot plate, shelves for dishes and groceries, a closet, and a bed which hung on the back of the bathroom door. I went to the dime store where I bought a few pots and pans as well as a little oven in which I could make some biscuits. Dan and Jerd remained with Mamie and Nat in Broomfield.

Mother Baldwin sent us $50.00 per month as long as we needed it. The day before Thanksgiving we had no food in the house as Mother Baldwin usually sent her check around the first of the month. When I went to the mailbox which was located in the front hall of the apartment building, I found a $50.00 check from Daddy. Since the mail came late in the day, I wouldn't be able to cash it until Friday. However, the care-taker was nice enough to loan me $5.00 until Friday. Then, the next day J.B. and I went to town and had our Thanksgiving dinner.

The day after Thanksgiving John and I went shopping as John wanted a new suit to wear to see the doctor. We had difficulty finding anything to fit him, and when we eventually found a suit that was long enough, it had to be practically remade. He told me that night that if he did not live through the operation, he wanted to be buried in his new suit.

I called and made an appointment for John to see Dr. O'Neal who had a large office downtown. The first of the week we took a streetcar to Dr. O'Neal's office building where John was to have his examination. The doctor examined him, gave him something for pain, and told him that he wanted to take some x-rays the next morning.

After the x-rays had been taken, Dr. O'Neal called in Dr. Perkins as a consultant as he was the one who was to perform the surgery. The date was set for January 6, 1916.

The night before the operation, J.B. was admitted to St. Luke's Hospital. He had told the doctors to please make sure that the bed was long enough. But, when I went in to see him, his feet were hanging way over the end of the bed. I went out to the nurse's station and complained whereupon the orderly remedied the situation by changing the side-rails on the bed.

The next day Nat came out "to walk the halls with me" while John was in surgery. He was a great comfort to me, and I don't know what I would have done without him. The operation lasted approximately five hours, but it seemed more like ten hours. When the doctor finally did appear, he told us that J.B. had come through the operation all right. For that I was grateful. They had found a mass in his intestines which could not be removed. They had made a straight gut in his intestines in order to by pass the mass. John would have approximately two years to live. I couldn't understand why it had to happen to him. He was such a good person, intelligent, and kind. He had so much to live for. Why him? From now on he would have to be very careful what he ate and could not have any carbohydrates at all. John would have to have extremely good care and would be in the hospital quite a while. He would have to have special private nurses around the clock. Miss Emory would be his day nurse and Miss Smith would be his night nurse.

Nat and I went down to the hospital cafeteria and had lunch. He brought me the sad news that Jerd had been hit by a car and hadn't made it. My poor little Jerd. He had been such a pleasure to me on our long journey but I would miss him terribly.

John was extremely ill but slowly continued to improve. He stayed in the hospital until March. The nurses were so very nice to me, and occasionally, I would go relieve Miss Emory during supper. Sometimes she would return with a dinner tray. When I inquired as to how much I owed for the dinner, I was told that I didn't owe anything. The patient that was to receive this dinner had already been discharged that afternoon.

When the nurse would start to fluff his pillow he would say, "Let my wife do that. She can do it so much better." That made me feel badly as I knew that I had to depend on them. However, they seemed to take it with a grain of salt.

When John was well enough to leave the hospital, I rented a furnished three-room brick house on Logan Boulevard for $15.00 per month. It was located just outside the city limits. There was a large grassy back yard and barn where Dan could stay and a sleeping porch where John could be in the open.

We lived close to a grocery store and a drug store. The druggist was Dr. Mattox. When J.B. became well enough to walk, he would walk up to the drug store. He and Dr. Mattox became good friends. Mrs. Mattox had two nephews. One was Joe Allen and the other's name was Bob.

One afternoon while I was in the drug store a young woman spoke to me. She had fair complexion, short dark hair, and a round face. She was a violinist and her father was a cellist with a symphony orchestra there in Denver. Her name was Grace Miller and she proved to be a lifelong friend.

About this time we received word that Mr. Andrew Johnson had decided to move to the Imperial Valley in California. As Nat wasn't planning to accompany him, he and Mamie decided to move back to Osceola, Arkansas. While enroute from Broomfield to Osceola, Mamie, Nat, and baby Eunice stopped and spent the night with us on our sleeping porch.

Around the last of June, Joe came over to talk to us. He and his cousin owned a cabin in the Rockie Mountain reserve near Bear Creek Canyon. The cabin was about sixteen miles from Evergreen which was the nearest community. Joe invited us to spend the rest of the summer there with them if I would do the cooking, whereupon we accepted his offer. There would be no charge.

──Bear Creek Canyon──

I packed up the buggy and we prepared to leave for the cabin around the first of July. Later, that day we came upon a little settlement. There was a large sign across the road that said, "Damned if I know." When we inquired as to why this settlement was named, "Damned if I know," we were told that people passing through were always asking questions as to how far they were from different places. So, they put up a sign to save people the trouble of asking.

The scenery near Bear Creek Canyon was just beautiful. The Colorado white pines were tall and numerous. Here, fishing was excellent and the beautiful speckled trout were plentiful. John caught as many as 40 of them in one afternoon. Joe and Bob went hunting nearly every day and brought in squirrel, gross, prairie hens, or rabbits.

Around the first week of August, John suggested that I write to Grace and ask her to come for a visit. I did and she came for a week. I thoroughly enjoyed her stay, especially while John fished and Joe and Bob hunted.

We rented a post office box in Evergreen. We would check to see whether we had any mail and buy supplies whenever we went into Evergreen.

One afternoon upon arriving there I went to buy a newspaper as I usually did when buying supplies. The headlines of the Denver Post read, "Asheville Washed Away." The French Broad River had overflowed its banks and had done a lot of damage in that section of the state. I was very concerned about my family and wrote to Daddy as soon as I could. He sent a telegram saying that everyone was all right. Most of the working farm was damaged, but no one was injured. Jim had had the best crop he had ever had, but now it was totally ruined. Of course, I was relieved to hear that everyone at home was well. But, poor Jim, all that hard work for nothing. It was terrible to think that Jim's beautiful green crop was totally destroyed.

In September we returned to Denver where John visited his doctor and we prepared for the last leg of our trip into New Mexico. Our destination this time was Roswell. John's sister, Mary, had remarried and was living in Roswell with her husband, Will Casey. In this leg of our journey we were to do no camping as John was not well enough, so we gave our camping equipment to Joe and Bob. Most of the nights we were to spend either in hotels or at ranch houses.

Joe's dog had puppies and Joe gave me one as a gift. I named this tiny white chow puppy, Joe, after him. We were to take him with us on our trip.

— New Mexico Bound —

On September 6, 1916, we started on our trip to New Mexico. We spent the first night in Pueblo, Colorado. We had been told that we had better get an early start the next morning as there would be no water for fifty miles. We did and about 7:00 P.M. the next night, we rode into Walsenburg.

We always carried a gallon jug of water with us. When we had a drink, we gave Dan a drink, too. The hotel where we stayed the previous night always packed us a picnic lunch.

One afternoon we ate our lunch on the divide which was the top of the mountain between Colorado and New Mexico. It took us all afternoon to get down the mountain, and we spent the night that night at Raton, New Mexico which was located at the foot of the mountain.

We were told at the hotel that we would not be allowed to take the dog upstairs with us. He would have to stay in the basement. So, we waited until later that night when everything was quiet. The, J.B. quietly crept down the back stairs to the basement, found the dog, brought him back upstairs, and put him in bed with us where he slept all night.

Around noon of the next day we came to a cowboy camp and were invited to dinner. There was no sign of food, but a pot of beans with a lid over it had been placed in a hole in the ground and a fire built of cow chips over it to make it hot. To go with the beans we were given some sour dough bread. That was the only night that we camped, and we slept on a blanket on the ground all night long.

One night we spent in Antonchica, New Mexico, where only one white man lived. All others were Mexican. As we approached this little town, it looked from a distance as though it were a town of red tile roofs. But on our arrival there we found it to be red pepper strung across the roofs to such an extent that it left the appearance of red tile roofs even from a short distance away. Here, we had a pleasant stay of several days with a beautiful Mexican woman. She was tall and slender and very hospitable. Her home was an old large one-story dwelling made of doby. J.B. thought that if might have been built there when the Spanish occupied New Mexico.

On the morning which we were to leave I awoke to see a huge tarantula on the ceiling in the corner above the bed. I didn't move for fear that I would waken J.B. When he finally awoke, I pointed the tarantula out to him. He said, "Let's get out of here." The lady had prepared our breakfast and a nice picnic lunch. We thanked her for her gracious hospitality and continued on our way.

On J.B.'s 31st birthday, the 22nd of September, we rode into Roswell. Mother Baldwin was there visiting Mary. Everyone was glad to see us as they were not expecting to see us this soon.

Around the first week of October we learned through Mary that the doctor at Hope, New Mexico, Dr. Yokum, wanted to go away for several weeks to study at the University of Rochester, in Rochester, New York. He came to see us to talk about John's taking over his practice for him while he was gone. Of course, this was the break that John had been waiting for, and he immediately agreed to carry on for him until he returned.

We drove Dr. and Mrs. Yokum to the station in their car to catch the train, and even though it was night we headed immediately for Hope. As there were no clearly defined roads to follow, we were not long in realizing that we had passed the same shepherd's house three times and we were going around in circles. By this time it was two o'clock in the morning, so we stopped as we were almost frozen from the cold. The shepherd built a blazing fire to keep us warm and gave us something hot to drink. I must have looked totally exhausted; so, the shepherd spread up his bed for me and allowed me to lie down and rest awhile. J.B. covered me up with his heavy long overcoat, and I went sound asleep and slept until daylight.

We finally arrived in Hope, New Mexico. The doctor and his wife had left their house completely furnished, and we stayed in their home the whole time we were there.

While at Hope we experienced a measles epidemic from which we made enough money to buy a new black Ford car after we returned to Roswell. It was called a tin Lizzie. We were very proud of our new purchase. For it we paid $405.00 cash, and we took great pride in keeping it shined and polished like new.

At the end of six weeks Dr. and Mrs. Yokum returned to Hope by train, and J.B. began his report to the Dr. concerning his patients. Dr. Yokum asked me to go on duty with a patient of his. An old man fell off of a windmill and was seriously injured. His back was broken and he was to be taken to the Catholic Hospital in Roswell as there was no hospital in Hope. Roswell was fifty miles away and there was nothing between Hope and Roswell except for cactus, tumbleweed, and sheep. I rode in the ambulance with the patient and stayed with him during the daytime. But, when night came, I walked back to Mary's house and usually arrived in time for supper. The sisters wore brown habits and were very good to me while I was there. Three days later the man died, and J.B. returned to Roswell from Hope by train. When I called Dr. Yokum to inform him of the man's death, he told me that he would like for me to come back to Hope to nurse a stroke victim who had contracted pneumonia. This was around the middle of November. While I was in route to Hope by train I heard that Woodrow Wilson had been re-elected president. Dr. Yokum met me at the station. I stayed with the patient 24 hours a day, but I was officially on duty with him only at night. His wife cared for him during the daytime.

One morning the woman told me, "Now, you go to bed early this morning because we are going to have a special supper tonight. The men are going out to kill some sheep, and we will have mutton stew." I was hungry and thoroughly enjoyed the meal as I had never had mutton stew before. It was a treat for me. However, sometime during the night I became dreadfully ill, and these people did not have indoor facilities.

The next morning I told the woman that I wasn't feeling well and that I was going to walk up to Dr. Yokum's office. I had a terrible cold. While talking to the doctor I said, "I am ill. I have a terrible cold." Whereupon he examined me and said, "Mrs. Baldwin, you don't have a cold. You're pregnant."

I responded, "I just feel terrible. I became ill last night. I guess I must have eaten too much."

He laughed and said, "Well, you'll have something to tell the doctor."

I couldn't go back to the patient and I just wasn't able. Dr. Yokum said, "You may stay at our house until J.B. can come after you."

He put me to bed and gave me some medicine. J.B. took the train to Hope and took me back to Roswell with him where we spent Christmas with Mary, Bill, and Mother Baldwin.

Around the end of January, 1917, we discovered that there was a medical practice open at Lovington, New Mexico, due to the fact that all the doctors had gone to war. The First World War had just begun. This opening we decided to take. And, in February, after picking up enough second hand furniture to suffice, we engaged a truck to move us, including Dan. We drove our new Ford.

Between Roswell and Cap Rock there was no water at all. Cap Rock just about breaks New Mexico in the middle. As one approaches the huge rock, there seems to be no opening whatsoever through it. But, as one gets near he discovers that there is a small opening which leads through to Pole Cat Canyon. Here, the land is green with mesquite, and the well is nearby. We spent the night there at a log cabin motel which was large enough for several rooms, a dining room, and kitchen. The only man we saw the whole time we were there was a jolly black man named Bill who did the cooking. He did provide wonderful meals. There was a large weeping willow tree on the front lawn. From Pole Cat Canyon it is fifty miles before drinking water can again be found.

Soon after we arrived in Lovington. This was a new cattle town of approximately 100 people. Many houses were made of doby, but the bank was covered with tin and marked like brick. There was a two-story grocery store with a large front porch on the upper level surrounded by a railing. This provided a covered walkway underneath on the street.

Soon, we found that there was no place where we could stay, except the hotel. But, within a few days we were able to rent a shoe shop building where we stayed for a while. An article appeared in the newspaper saying that Dr. and Mrs. Baldwin were residing in the old shoe shop. Upon reading this, I cried and cried for I never thought that I would have to live in a shoe shop.

I had brought enough bedding from home for the cots and the bed J.B. had bought. The shop had been clean when we moved in. We placed our hot plate upon the bar where shoes had once been laid. Here is where we prepared our breakfast. As we didn't have a table, the cot sufficed. Mary had given us some dishes. However, we ate our other meals at the hotel.

In a few weeks a pool room over a grocery store went out of business. We rented the pool room, put in some partitions, and fixed the place up to the point where it was livable. Here, we remained the rest of the time we were in Lovington.

Behind one partition was the doctor's office and behind another was his operating room. We made up one area for our bedroom. The kitchen was down at the end of the hall. There was no bathroom in the building.

J.B. bought an ice box, a second handed oil stove for cooking, and a table for the kitchen. We used empty packing boxes turned upside down as shelves.

Doctor Culbertson, who lived next door to Mary, had given us a beautiful kneehole library desk as he was moving back to Kentucky. We placed this desk in the long hallway. The telephone was placed on the desk which was used as an appointment desk. This hall was to be used as a waiting room, and I had placed chairs there to accommodate the patients.

I couldn't understand how the sand could accumulate on the floor so quickly overnight. Every morning I would sweep the floor. But, by the next morning, little piles of sand would have accumulated there. J.B. told me that the little whirlwinds out in this part of the country caused that to occur.

One afternoon the entire sky suddenly became extremely black. I had washed my clothes and they were drying on the line behind the house. Upon seeing the dark sky, I presumed that I must hurry to take in my clothes before the rain storm came. As I was hurrying to take my clothes off the line, our neighbor, Mr. Hollyfield, called to me and asked, "Mrs. Baldwin, what are you doing?"

I answered, "I'm taking my clothes in before it rains."

He responded, "Mrs. Baldwin, you've been here too long to be a tenderfoot. There's no rain in that cloudy sky. It will bring only wind and sand."

Several days later, John received his first call. A man from Elida, a town about eighty miles away, came and asked John to go to see his wife. We started on the trip, but since the roads were sand which was continuously shifted by the wind, each car carried a shovel along with which to shovel out in case of getting stuck in the sand, a very common occurrence at that time. After a long trip that for once was without mishap, we finally reached the man's home which was an underground dugout with sacks on the floor for rugs.

The woman was soon restored to health, and the check which John received, since the fee in this area was $1.00 per mile for the trip regardless of the nature of the illness, started us on the road which we had traveled so far and at so many hazards to find.

One night around 6:00 P.M. J.B. received a call from a physician near Portales, which was also a small town about 80 miles away in the opposite direction from Elida. This physician was on a case and needed assistance. Therefore, he called J.B., and I went with him. During this time I always accompanied J.B. on all of his calls.

Upon arrival at the patient's home, we found that she and her husband also lived in a dugout. We went down some steps to find ourselves in what appeared to be a very comfortable home. There were expensive wool carpets on the floor and lovely furniture some of which was antiques. The interior was beautifully decorated with Indian tapestries covering the walls.

We found that the woman was having a very difficult delivery and was in convulsions. A well-wrapped sterling silver spoon was put between her teeth to prevent her from biting her tongue. On her bed was a beautiful fur blanket resembling a bear skin. The baby was eventually delivered only to find that it was stillborn. The woman eventually awakened and did seem better before morning.

The next day when we started home J.B. handed me the check for our night's work. It was for $80.00, and there were pictures of white-faced Herefords on the front of the check.

After returning to Lovington, J.B. immediately took the check to the bank to have it cashed whereupon the cashier told J.B. that the man who had given it to him had been exempt from the army to raise cattle for them.

Later, her husband brought his wife to J.B.'s office to be examined.

Late one night as we were returning home from a case, a wind storm suddenly came up. The sand was blowing terribly. Our white chow, Joe, was standing upon the back seat of the car looking out of the opened window which was made of isinglass. There was a sudden jolt whereupon Joe fell out of the window. We immediately stopped the car to retrieve our dog only to find him dead. He had broken his neck when he fell. We felt terrible about it as Joe had brought only pleasure to our lives. There was nothing we could do for him. J.B. dug his grave and buried him right there where he had fallen.

Not too long after that J.B. was called for another labor case. It was in a cabin this time. The cabin had dirt floors and an old stove which burned cow chips. The baby was delivered successfully, but the patient was very weak and died soon afterwards. The midwife had evidently failed to call the doctor in time to save the woman and that made J.B. furious. He cared very much about his patients. J.B. tried to stop the bleeding, but much to his dismay, he could not get it to stop. She bled to death, and there was nothing we could do to prevent it.

In April J.B. was becoming hesitant for me to accompany him on his calls as our baby was to be born around the middle of July. Therefore, he called his brother, Rodney, and asked him to come live with us for a while and accompany him on his calls. Rodney was living in Badin, N.C. at the time where he worked at the Alcoa Aluminum Plant. Rodney soon took the train to Roswell, New Mexico, and J.B. went after him as Roswell was a hundred miles away. Rodney managed to find employment at the grocery store downstairs which was convenient for us. From then on, Rodney did the driving for J.B.

Mother Baldwin had come back with Rodney and J. B. for a long visit. She was a tremendous help to me and helped me make baby clothes.

J.B. came home one night and asked me if I felt like going out that night and staying with a patient of his, a little girl approximately three years of age. The weather was chilly. The family lived about 18 miles away out in the country. Rodney would drive me out to the home and would come back for me when I was no longer needed. I agreed to go as the child was recovering from pneumonia and needed someone to watch over her for several nights. I would not have to do much except watch her sleep.

Just as the father was about to retire for the night he said, "Mrs. Baldwin, if the fire dies down tonight and you get cold, use this." He pointed to a tub of chips which was located behind the stove. "Also, I have a small amount of coal; but, please don't use it unless you have to. I think the chips will be sufficient for you to use tonight."

Then, the family members went to bed leaving me to keep watch over their sleeping child.

Sometime during the night I became cold. I looked and saw that the fire had died down. Then, I went over to the wash tub full of chips. When the father had previously mentioned the chips, I had thought that he was talking about wood chips. Upon closer examination, I saw that the tub was filled with dried cow chips, not wood chips as I had expected. Under no circumstances was I going to touch that. So, I went over to the coal and added some to the fire. Before morning I had burned it all.

When the family came downstairs the next morning, it didn't take the father long to detect that there was no fire and no coal. He said, "Why, Mrs. Baldwin, you've burned my coal."

I answered, "Well, you know I wasn't going to touch that stuff."

Every night that I stayed with the child, her father would come in carrying a large tub of cow chips. And, he would say, "Here's Mrs. Baldwin's fuel." After that I had no choice but to burn the chips as coal was expensive and cost about $5.00 a scuttle.

One warm night around the first of June Mother Baldwin became very ill with what J.B. thought to be appendicitis. J.B. immediately called a surgeon in Roswell and asked him to come to Lovington to assist him. Mary accompanied the surgeon from Roswell to Lovington. Mother Baldwin was operated on in our office. What J.B. had thought to be appendicitis turned out to be cancer. There was nothing they could do for her, and she died three days later, June 6, 1917. She was approximately 68 years of age.

We began preparation for the long journey by train to take Mother Baldwin's body back to Nicholasville, Kentucky for burial. I had to borrow a dress from Mrs. Hollyfield, my neighbor, as I had very few maternity clothes. Mary, Rodney, J.B., and I made the trip together. Mary did not want me to go as I was in my eighth month, but J.B. refused to leave me there. He did not want to take the chance of my having the baby alone. There was no other doctor in the vicinity.

Mary's husband, Will Casey, could not come with us. He was a shoe maker and made beautiful cowboy boots by hand. He could not leave his shop.

We changed trains in Danville, Kentucky, and went from there to Nicholasville. J.B. had lots of friends, some of which invited us to stay with them.

After the funeral, J.B. said, "Since we are this close to Greenlee, we'll go home to visit your family for a few days." We took the train but stopped over in Coal Creek, Tennessee, to see some friends. After spending the night in the hotel, we again resumed our journey to Greenlee where we stayed three days visiting. We found everyone to be well. My brother, Leland, had been married the previous January to Mae Lewis of Maryville, Tennessee. They had been living in Badin, N.C. where Leland had been working for the Alcoa Aluminum Co.

After three days we again resumed our journey by train to return to New Mexico. We took the local train to Asheville where we boarded the Carolina Special. While we had been visiting my family in Greenlee, N. C., Rodney had traveled to Louisville, Kentucky, to visit his twin children, Nancy and Louis Findley Baldwin, who were approximately 12 or 14 years of age. Rodney was divorced from his wife, Marie, who had remarried and had custody of their children. When the train stopped at Louisville, Kentucky, Rodney joined us for our return trip. This was the first time I had had an opportunity to meet Nancy and Louis.

One July morning I was sitting at the breakfast able when my bag of waters broke. Just then, the telephone rang. It was a labor case in Cap Rock which was approximately fifty miles away. They had to have the doctor right away. Before departing for Cap Rock, J.B. left me 1/4th of a grain of morphine in capsule form. He said, "Now, if the pains start before I return, be sure and take this." Then, he left to deliver someone else but did return that night just before dark. I told him that I had had no pain while he had been gone. As it was against the law for a doctor to deliver his own wife, J.B. wanted someone else to be with us when the baby came. So, he said, "I guess I had better go get Grandma Andrews and our neighbor, Mrs. Hollyfield. Around 9:00 PM. On July 16, 1917, I was delivered of a beautiful little baby girl who weighed exactly 6 lbs.

The next morning Rodney came in to look at the tiny baby I held in my arms and said, "She's so little and pretty. Let's name her Pansy."

J.B., who had just walked in the door, responded, "Hell, no! We're not going to have any six foot pansy around this house. Her name is Mary. I've had her named for a long time, now."

Grandma Andrews stayed with us for about three days. Then, her son received word that he had been called into the army, and, she had to leave. J.B. paid her with a $20.00 gold piece.

J.B. wouldn't let me get up out of bed. Rodney did the cooking and brought my meals tome on a tray. J.B. would bring me a pan of water and other necessities that I would need in order to bathe and change the baby.

In August there was a big rodeo, and the town was packed with people. The only hotel in town was full. It was during this time that J.B. stayed out all night one rainy night and did not return home until the following night. In that part of the country it didn't rain often, but that night the rain just poured down in torrents. Rodney and I were worried sick as J.B. had never done anything like that before. The old pain was beginning to return. Dr. Perkins in Denver had told me when he operated on J.B. a year and a half previous to that that my husband would have approximately two years to live. I could see his strength grow less with every passing day.

When J.B. did return home, he was not drunk, but I could tell that he had been drinking heavily. He had not had a drink since his operation as the doctor had told him not to drink. He had been playing poker with some big gamblers in Cap Rock and had lost a lot of money. However, when J.B. gambled, he never went into debt. He knew that he wouldn't live long, and he had previously made me a promise that he would never gamble more than he had in his pockets. When I put him to bed the next night, all I found in his trousers were a nickel and a penny.

However, instead of telling me the truth about losing, J.B. made up a story to tell me. He said, "I won a lot of money playing poker with some friends in Cap Rock. But, I was so exhausted that I fell asleep at the cabin and someone stole all of my winnings." Of course, I didn't believe John's story, but I never let him know that. I pretended to believe him.

Two or three days later J.B. came home and laid a check for $300.00 on the kitchen table. He said, "I've sold Dan. Here's the check for $300.00." He had sold him to Mr. Hollyfield, our neighbor, who had a little girl. I suppose that he wanted a tame horse for her. I didn't cry, but neither did I go down to say goodbye to him as I was afraid that I would cry. I knew that the Hollyfield's were good people and would give Dan good care. He looked as beautiful as he always had. They took Dan out to the country, and I never saw him again.

Not long after that J.B. told me that he would just have to go back to Denver as he was suffering so much that he just couldn't work. Around the first of November he did go back to Denver to see the doctors. Rodney and I stayed there until just before Thanksgiving when we went to Mary's. We left early one frosty morning. The grey coyotes looked beautiful running across the frozen ground. Rodney commented that they looked as if they were in a hurry. Perhaps their feet were frozen.

After Thanksgiving Rodney and I went back to Lovington to pack up all of our belongings. I packed my trunk, all the lovely fine china which Mary had given us, the doctor's books and instruments, as well as everything else. While we were in the midst of packing, Mr. Hollyfield and another man came to present me with a gift from the residents of Lovington, $178.00. There was a letter signed by all 100 residents. I was deeply touched. Mary and Mr. Hollyfield told me not to worry about our belongings. Rodney and I were to leave them there for the time being and Mary and Mr. Hollyfield would ship them later by truck across the desert to Roswell.

As I had no shoes fit to wear, I had to go downtown shopping. I looked all over town but was unable to find anything suitable as my feet were too long and narrow. Most of the shoes I tried on were too short and broad. I finally found a pair that I could wear; however, they were too tight and hurt my feet. I also bought the baby a white flannel coat and warm cap to match.

—— Return to Denver ——

Rodney took Mary and me to the train station on the night of January 11, 1918. Rodney carried our one little suitcase, and I carried Mary, a pillow, and my purse. He saw us to our Pullman and kissed us goodbye. We were now on our way back to Denver.

I put Mary to bed and then I went to sleep. When I awoke the next morning, the train was still. There was no one around except the black porter, Mary, and me. I asked him, "Where is everyone? Where are we?"

He said, "We're froze up. The trains froze up. This is Clovis, New Mexico. Everyone else is over to the 'Harvey House' 'cross the rails eaten' breakfast."

Would you please watch the baby and see that she doesn't fall off the bed while I go across the street to get something to eat? I would appreciate it very much."

He answered, "Of course, I'll take care of her."

"Thank you," I said, whereupon I went across the street.

I returned about an hour later to find that the porter had made up the bed. Mary was awake and being entertained by him.

In approximately two hours time, the train was on its way again. We only had to change trains once and that was at Amarilla, Texas, which is located in the panhandle.

When we left Amarilla around 4:00 P.M. on the same day, the air was thick with snow. A couple of inches had already accumulated. I had the baby and pillow in one arm and the suitcase in the other, plus my purse and tickets. I thought that I would never get to the right train. Someone was kind enough to help me. A nice young man picked up my suitcase and carried it to the train for me.

When we finally reached it, we boarded, but the conductor informed me that Mary and I would have to travel in an upper berth as there was no lower berth available. I didn't see how I would be able to manage in an upper berth with the baby. She could easily fall off. Fortunately, a very nice traveling salesman from the other side of the train spoke up and said, "I'll change with her. I have a lower berth." I was so appreciative and thanked him for his generosity.

We finally settled down and the baby fell asleep right away as she was exhausted from the journey. I asked the nice salesman if he would be kind enough to watch the baby while I went to the dining car for supper, and he agreed to do this for me.

When I awoke on the morning of January 13, I found that it was still snowing. The snow was so deep that the train had stopped, and the snow plows had to dig us out. When I went to the dining car for breakfast, I asked someone where we were. The reply was, "Somewhere in God's country," as we were in Colorado by this time. We remained here until around noontime when the train began to move again.

The train finally pulled into the Denver station around 5:00P.M. I hailed a taxi and went to St. Luke's Hospital. J. B. was just as angry as he could be. He had been extremely worried about us, and I hadn't called or wired him from the train. However, he was glad to see us and soon forgave me.

Someone at the hospital was able to find me a room about a block up the street with two elderly Danish ladies. They were extremely good to the baby and me. They took their clothes basket in which they made a bed for the baby and were good enough to keep her for me during the daytime while I was with my husband.

I talked with Dr. O'Neal who seemed to think that J. B. would do just as well out of the hospital as he was now doing in the hospital. He was becoming restless and irritable.

Therefore, I left Mary with the ladies and went out in search of another room. I walked and walked. Everywhere I went I heard, "We will not rent to sick people of those who have children." Of course, I had both.

A few days later Dr. O'Neal called me and asked me to come to his office for a consultation. He said, "Your husband will not live very long. I think that two or three weeks will be the most that you could hope for. I understand that you come from the mountains of North Carolina, and I don't think that it would be wise for you to continue to say here with a baby, a dying husband, and no money. If I were you I would take him home to my family while he's still alive. A live body is less expensive to take home that a dead one. You need to be with your family members right now anyway. Besides, I understand that Asheville is a health resort and a very nice place."

I said, "I would be glad to do that if J. B. will go willingly."

"I think he will," he responded.

When I returned to the hospital, I found that Mary was there talking to J.B.

I said, "I've been to see Dr. O'Neal."

He answered, "He's been here, too. He told me that he thought everything would be easier on you if we went back to Greenlee, and I think so, too."

I said, "Well, when do you want to start?"

He replied, "Right away."

First, I went downtown to a pawn shop to sell my valuable diamond ring in order to get enough money to purchase the tickets for our trip. Mary gave me extra money and told me that she would pay the hospital bill. I then went to the ticket office to purchase our train tickets.

Mary stayed with J.B. at the hospital while I went back to my boarding house and packed my suitcase. The baby and I were to take a taxi to the train station as J. B. was to go by ambulance. Our train was to leave Denver at 9:00P.M., February 1, 1918.

—— Homeward Bound ——

After arriving at the station, I waited and waited for the ambulance which I thought would never come. I was beginning to worry that the ambulance had possibly become stuck in the snow. The conductor was very impatiently walking up and down saying, "You're holding up the train."

When the ambulance finally arrived, the driver informed us, "We would have been here sooner, but the engine was frozen." The ambulance personnel took J. B. to our drawing room on a stretcher and tried to make him comfortable on the lower berth. I put the baby in the upper berth surrounded by pillows as I was terrified that she would fall out. The porter then made up the little couch for me to sleep on. Mostly, the ride was smooth.

The First World War was still being fought. In war time when the armed forces needs a train for its troops, they put the passenger train on a side track and take the engine. Several times during our trip home, we were put on one of these side tracks.

The following night we ate supper in St. Joseph, Missouri. The porter was nice enough to bring us our meals on a tray, and the food was delicious. However, J. B. was weak and ate very little.

Two mornings later we awoke to find that we were in Kansas City, Missouri. The train was still, and we stayed there all day. However, they continued to bring us our meals. As it was easier to bathe J.B. and the baby while the train was still, I gave them their baths. After supper the train began to move again.

The next lay-over was in Louisville, Kentucky. Right across the street from the depot was a hotel. Since I knew that we would be there for approximately twelve hours, I went over and rented a room. I returned to our drawing room with a wheel chair and a red cap and prepared to move us to the hotel for the day as I knew that it would be a change for J.B. and he would be able to rest better. The train would not depart again until about 9:00P.M. that night.

We went from Louisville to Danville, Kentucky where we had to change trains and take the Carolina Special. It was dark and I found this difficult as we had to wait for about an hour or an hour and a half in the depot. By this time we were all very tired and glad when the Special finally came.

When we awoke the next morning in Harriman, Tennessee, the train was still again. This time, the only car that had been left was ours. As we were out in the country, the porter had to go to a little food stand right down the road in order to bring us our food. We stayed there all day. Around dusk another train came along and picked us up. We were finally moving again.

The next stop was Knoxville where they again put us off on a side track and we spent the night. The next morning I asked the porter to watch the baby as I was familiar with Knoxville and knew where I could find good meals. I found my way to 'The Busy Bee' where I ate my meals that day and brought something back for J.B. around 3:00P.M. another train came along and picked us up. We finally arrived in Asheville before dusk. I was just getting off the train, and J. B. and the baby were still in the berth. Suddenly I happened to recognize my friend Harry from the Donahue and Hall Funeral Home. I hadn't forgotten that during my days of nurse's training, he had continually teased me about marrying such a tall man. As he had told me in jest that he would bury my husband for me, I passed him by and could not speak to him. The pain was just too great.

I had the porter bring J. B. in a wheel chair to a taxi. The driver recommended a new hotel in town, The George Vanderbilt Hotel where he proceeded to drive us. As I was about to register us in a room there, the clerk looked at the baby, my husband, and me and suddenly shouted, "Get that man out of here! We'll have no sick people and no babies in this hotel!"

I said, "May I please use the phone?"

He answered, "Yes."

I then called the Langreen Hotel. I explained to the man on the other end of the phone, "I have a sick husband and tiny baby. I am now at the George Vanderbilt Hotel, and they have refused to let me register here. They say that they don't take sick people and babies at this hotel. I live in Greenlee. I have just arrived here by train, and the other train, Old #12, has already left. I have to spend the night.

The man answered, "You may bring your husband here, and I'll have the room ready when you arrive."

When we arrived at the Langreen Hotel, we had a very nice room on the mezzanine floor. There was a lovely view from the balcony. The manager had provided me with a porter who helped me bathe my husband and put him to bed. The porter then brought us our supper on a tray.

The next morning the porter was kind enough to watch the baby while I went to town to buy J.B. a new shirt, tie, and some underwear. We had been traveling for seven days and nights and all of our clothes were dirty. I returned to find the porter rocking the baby. He had shaved J.B. and had him ready to put on his new clothes.

───── *Home at Last* ─────

Old #12 left Asheville around 2:00P.M. on Thursday, February 7, 1918, and was due to arrive at Greenlee around 4:00PM. Daddy and Polly met us at the depot with a horse drawn buggy. The porter helped J.B. into the buggy. He sat up tall and straight, looking so stately in his derby hat. Then, I handed the baby to him, and Daddy climbed up into the driver's seat. As the buggy had only two seats, Polly had ridden one of the horses for us to ride home. I rode home side saddle with Polly behind me on the horse's back. J.B. and I were so exhausted. When we finally arrived at home, I gave the baby to Mother and put J.B. to bed.

The next morning my husband seemed better. He ate a good breakfast, and I bathed him. I had to give him a hypodermic. Dr. O'Neal had given me enough morphine to last until he died, and I had to give him some every three hours.

Our neighbors and friends began coming in. Dr. J.B. Johnson came, also, to see if there was anything that he could do. He had married my cousin, Lillian Burgin, whose mother lived not too far away. Dr. Johnson was now practicing medicine at Greenlee.

J.B. gradually became worse and was in terrible pain. He couldn't talk much or swallow very well. I thought that lemon juice might help; so Mother sent Jack to the store to buy some lemons.

My brother, Leland, and sister-in law, Mae, were there as they had just buried their baby the week before. Francis Leland Greenlee, Jr. had been born November 22, 1917, and died February 2, 1918, of pneumonia following whooping cough. He was a beautiful baby with dark curly hair and had died at my brother's house in Badin, N.C. The night he died the director of P.J. Huneycutt's Funeral Home had to come seven miles from Albemarle, N.C. over a dirt road through sleet and ice to the Greenlee home in Badin. He brought the little casket with him as the roads were so bad that the child had to be embalmed at the Greenlee home. Then, the trip to Greenlee, N.C. for burial was an arduous one.

A funeral service for little Leland was held at the Greenlee home in McDowell County where one of my father's sister's Sarah Lenoir Greenlee, whom we called Aunt Lennie, sang, "Safe in the Arms of Jesus." Aunt Lennie was a painter and a proof reader and writer for "Harper's Bazaar" and "The Ladies Home Journal." Then, the two mile trip up the mountain for burial was begun as the Greenlee family cemetery was located on top of a mountain. It was snowing and there was difficulty getting up the dirt road to the cemetery. The scenery from the hilltop was beautiful as everything was white.

Monday night my husband worsened. As he was getting tired of the featherbed on which he was lying, Mother made up a cot which she and Jack placed in front of the fireplace. J.B. seemed more comfortable on the cot. I sat down beside him on a little stool and held his hand.

On Tuesday J.B.'s condition continued to worsen. Mae put Mary on the big double bed, gave her her first piece of chewing gum, and proceeded to teach Mary how to chew gum. She didn't swallow it, but chewed it like a lady.

J.B. died Tuesday night, February 13, 1918. I was kneeling beside the cot holding his hand when he died. I had talked to him for a long time. He looked at me, told me he loved me, and said, "Babe, it's all over."

The next morning we called Mr. Blanton of Blanton's Funeral Home in Marion, N.C. There was difficulty in finding a casket long enough for him, and Leland had to go with Mr. Blanton to High Point for one. A funeral service was held at home for J.B. Mae stayed with the baby while we went to the cemetery for the burial. J.B. was buried near little Leland at the Greenlee family cemetery at the top of the mountain. It was a clear day but the snow was frozen hard and crusty. The path up the mountain was mired in mud and climbing it was difficult at that point in my life it seemed to me that the best part of my life was ending. Little did I know that actually it was just beginning. I was just beginning a career of nursing for the public which was to last for 60 years before my retirement in 196. I loved my work and the people I worked for, and I had a young daughter to consider whose welfare was very precious to me.

Printed in the United States
by Baker & Taylor Publisher Services